VLADIMIR KEILIS-BOROK:

A BIOGRAPHY

1921-2013

Ori Books

Vladimir Keilis-Borok: A Biography

Editor: Anna Kashina

Copyright © 2014 by Ori Books

Ori Books is an imprint of Dragonwell Publishing
(www.dragonwellpublishing.com)

ISBN 978-1-940076-59-1

VLADIMIR KEILIS-BOROK
July 31, 1921—October 19, 2013

V. I. Keilis-Borok (1921-2013) is the founder of computational seismology and the pioneer of advance predictions of critical events in complex systems, including earthquakes, presidential elections, economic recessions, surges of unemployment, and crime waves. Among successful advance earthquake predictions made under his guidance are Irpinia earthquake in Italy (1980), Loma Prieta earthquake in California (1989), Chile earthquake of 2010, Japan earthquake of 2011, and many others.

V. I. Keilis-Borok developed new paradigms in the study of structure and dynamics of solid Earth. His trademark style involved exceptional organizational talent and insight that enabled him to make seemingly impossible connections between different fields of research and different groups of experts, often breaking the barriers between high theory, numerical modeling, and data analysis.

His outstanding achievements are recognized by memberships in many academies and international scientific organizations, including National Academy of Sciences of the USA, Academy of Sciences of the USSR, Pontifical Academy of Sciences, Academia Europea, Royal Astronomical Society, and others, as well as through awards and honors, and by the respect and devotion he inspired in his friends and colleagues.

This book contains his brief biography and reflections by his family, friends, and colleagues—a tribute to this truly remarkable man.

What was he like?

- He never followed rules
- He always questioned himself
- He was never bored
- He had a gift of seeing both the essence of matter and the big picture at the same time
- He was constantly fascinated with things around him
- He connected with people on a deep emotional level
- He was always there to help anyone he could
- He had amazing memory for facts and quotes
- He loved the mountains
- He found comfort in books, movies, poetry, and art
- He was in awe of children
- He inspired love and devotion, even at a very old age
- He never gave up

TABLE OF CONTENTS

A Lifetime of Love

Anna Kashina, granddaughter:

When a man passes away, he leaves behind a lifetime of memories, feelings, and thoughts. Many of them sink into oblivion, others fade with time and eventually lose their original meaning. It is impossible to capture, or even summarize all of them in one book. However, it is possible to bring some of them back to life, to create small windows that could give a glimpse of the person behind.

This task becomes even harder when talking about a truly extraordinary man. What we remember of him are no more than fragments in the rich tapestry of his life, people he loved, memories he cherished. It seems so important—and so impossible—to keep together the threads of this tapestry, to treasure them, to piece them into an image others can see, to share it, to pass it on. To remember.

This book is meant to celebrate V. I. Keilis-Borok's life, to keep alive the tapestry of his life, to allow others a glimpse of this remarkable man, so brilliant, so full of warmth and love that it had reached everyone who had the fortune of meeting him, even if briefly.

He had been so many things for so many people. To me, he was a grandfather—and so much more. My relationship with him cannot possibly be summarized in this one word that captures no more than a blood tie. He was, and will always be, the closest friend I ever had, my true love, my soul mate, who taught me everything I am. I called him Volodya, and this name itself became his definition in the eyes of my friends and loved ones. He was *my Volodya*, and saying this means more than any relationship can possibly describe. Many of those who knew him well could resonate with this feeling, of sharing so many facets with him that putting it all into words doesn't seem like a feasible task.

A few days after Volodya passed away, a young reporter from a local newspaper called me to ask some questions for an article she was writing about him. She had never met Volodya, but with admirable resolve to capture some of his personal side, she kept quizzing me: "What was he like?" "What do you remember most about him?" "What did you do with him when you were a child?"

As simple as these questions seemed, they stunned me. How do you put a lifetime into a few words? How do you describe a person whose love, compassion, and superb mind left a trace in so many lives? How do you put a simple definition to what it meant growing up by his side, when he put all of himself into molding me as a human being, making me feel loved, cherished, and treasured so deeply that this confidence—along with the insecurity of being up to it—stayed with me for decades to come?

I cannot imagine a world without him. It is impossible to even consider that I will never hear his voice, never be able to discuss my problems with him, never watch our favorite "Sounds of Music" and "Pirates of Penzance" curled up in cozy armchairs side by side. He always said that talking was not necessary, that just sitting together and doing unrelated things was a form of interaction, perhaps deeper than a regular conversation. We did that a lot. We did that all the time when I visited him during his last weeks, when he could no longer talk, and I could never find enough words to tell him what he meant to me. I found some consolation in reading him the novel we wrote together when I was in high school, "In the Name of the Queen". I hoped he could remember, like I did, all the happy times that went into the work on this book. I also spent a lot of time sitting quietly by his side, holding his hand, wishing I could go back in time and tell him at least a fraction of the love I felt for him.

When he passed away, I had a feeling that the whole world cried with me. Echoes of this cry were coming in for days and weeks as we received warm condolences from all over the world, from close friends and colleagues, from people we barely knew or never even heard about. I cried over the phone when I called to deliver the news and heard strangers I had never met cry on the other end of the line. We exchanged e-mails, often warmer and more personal than I normally do even with my closest friends. Everyone knew his health was declining. Yet, it was so hard to accept that he was gone, as the things that reminded of him surrounded us, watched over us—as if these small things carried his warm thoughts. We all found our comfort in different ways. But we could never come to terms with it.

During these weeks it occurred to me that if I were to put one defining word to what he was like, this word would be "love". Love defined his existence on so many levels. He connected with people in a deep emotional way, which felt in many ways exactly like falling in love, with all the emotional closeness, the pain, and the withdrawal afterwards. Many of those who met him felt this love. Many remember the thrill of instantly becoming an object of his keen interest, when even complete strangers suddenly found themselves telling him

Anna Kashina and Volodya Keilis-Borok
Philadelphia, PA, winter 2004

3

very personal things about their lives and finding deep compassion and understanding they couldn't get from anyone else. We, his family, basked in his love, and it is unimaginable to think about living on without it.

I can only hope that some of this love would live on in our memories, capturing those bright spots that can weave a glimpse of the extraordinary man behind.

"It became clear for me that it is unrealistic to have a hope for the creation of a pure theory [of the turbulent flows of fluids and gases] closed in itself. Due to the absence of such a theory we have to rely upon the hypotheses obtained by processing of the experimental data."

A. N. Kolmogorov

Our goal is not explaining the origin of extreme events, but identifying their observable precursors. We introduce an exactly solvable simple model which provides an analytical description of premonitory patterns. Independently of a specific process leading to the extreme event, these patterns emerge as the probability of an extreme event is rising; this applies also to processes involving inverse cascades too. Such patterns have been heuristically observed in real-life and modeled processes, including seismicity, percolation, and fluids dynamics.

The above results seem to be very consequential for integrating research in predictability of different natural disasters; for example, extended universality; candidate for control parameter, etc.

V. I. Keilis-Borok

Timeline

Based on the "Brief Bibliography of V.I. Keilis-Borok" published by the Russian Academy of Sciences, 2001:

Born: July 31, 1921, Moscow, Russia

1938   Graduated from high school (with honors)

1938-1943   Student, Moscow S. Orjonikidze Institute of Geological Prospecting

1943   Graduated from Moscow S. Orjonikidze Institute of Geological Prospecting (with honors)

1943   Junior Researcher, Central Research Laboratory of the Geophysical Trust, Narkomneft'.

1943-1989   The O.Yu. Shmidt Institute of Physics the Earth of the Academy of Sciences of the USSR (before 1960, Geophysical Institute of the Academy of Sciences of the USSR): 1943-1948, Graduate Student; 1948-1951, Junior Researcher; 1951-1963, Senior Researcher; 1953-1963, Leader, Group of Theoretical Seismology; 1963-1969, Chair, Laboratory of Methods of Interpretation of Seismic Observations; 1969-1989, Chair, Department of Computational Geophysics

1949   Ph.D., "Investigation of the Wavering of the Free Boundary of the Resistant Half-Space under the Influence of the Point Source"

1954   Doctor of Science, "Interference Seismic Waves in Layered Environment"

1957	The XI General Assembly of the International Union of Geodesy and Geophysics (IUGG), Canada
1958	Meeting of the European Seismological Committee, Holland
1959	Meeting for the control of nuclear tests, Switzerland
1960	Geneva meeting on seismic detection of nuclear explosions
1960-1980	Member, United Nations expert group on the ban of nuclear testing
1963	IUGG XIII General Assembly, USA
1964-1979	Chair, Committee on Mathematical Geophysics, the Academy of Sciences of the USSR
1965	Professor, Seismology
1965	Visiting scientist and lecturer, Aldermaston Research Center, UK
1965	Symposia on the theory and computational methods of the studies of the upper Earth mantle, Israel
1966	III International Symposium on the computational methods in geophysics, UK
1966-2013	Editor in Chief, "Computational Seismology"
1969-2013	Member, American Academy of Arts and Sciences
1970	"For Valiant Labor" Medal, commemorating 100 years since V. I. Lenin's birth
1971-2013	Member, National Academy of Sciences, USA
1975	Medal "Sign of Honor", USSR: for outstanding achievements in Soviet science and in connection with 250 years of the Academy of Sciences of the USSR

1978,1979	Fairchild Distinguished Scholar, California Institute of Technology, USA
1979-1983	Vice-President, International Association of Seismology and Physics of the Earth Interior (IASPEI)
1987-2013	Full Member, Russian Academy of Sciences (before 1991, Academy of Sciences of the USSR)
1987-1991	President, IUGG
1987-1993	Member, International Council for Science (ICSU)
1989-2013	Member, Royal Astronomical Society, UK
1990-1998	Director, International Institute of Earthquake Predictions Theory and Mathematical Geophysics of the Russian Academy of Sciences (MITPAN)
1990-1998	Chair, Scientific Council on Computational Geophysics, Russian Academy of Sciences
1990-2001	Member, since 1992—Chair, Scientific Council of the Russian Academy of Sciences on the International Decade for Natural Disaster Reduction
1992-2013	Member, Austrian Academy of Sciences
1992-1997	Member, Scientific Council of the International Association for the Promotion of Cooperation with Scientists from the New Independent States of the Former Soviet Union (INTAS)
1992-2002	Member, Bureau of the Division of Geology, Geophysics, Geochemistry, and Geological Sciences of the Russian Academy of Sciences
1992-2004	Member, Committee of Government Awards of the Russian Federation
1993-1999	Member, Russian Foundation of Fundamental Research
1994-2013	Member, Pontifical Academy of Sciences, Vatican

1994-2002	Co-chair, Russian-American working group on earthquake predictions
1995-2013	Doctor Honoris Causa, Institut de Physique du Globe, Paris, France
1996-2004	Council Member, Pontifical Academy of Sciences, Vatican
1997-2002	Committee Member "Scientists for International Safety and Arms Control", Russian Academy of Sciences
1998	Medal of Friendship, Russian Federation: for outstanding service to the government, many years of labor, and key contributions to the strengthening of friendship and cooperation between nations.
1998	Lewis Fry Richardson Medal, European Geosciences Union: for research in the areas of non-linear dynamics
1998-2013	Principal Investigator, MITPAN
1998-2013	Member, Scientific Council "High-productivity Computational Systems and Their Applications", Russian Academy of Sciences
1999-2002	Member, Coordinating Council on Earth Sciences, Russian Academy of Sciences
1999-2013	Member, Academia Europea
1999-2010	Professor-in-Residence, Institute of Geophysics and Planetary Physics, University of California, Los Angeles, USA
2010-2013	Professor Emeritus, Department of Earth, Space, and Planetary Sciences, University of California, Los Angeles, USA

V. I. Keilis-Borok's Achievements

Prepared by Vladimir I. Keilis-Borok and Alexander A. Soloviev:

The major part of Keilis-Borok's studies concerns dynamics and structure of the solid Earth, with focus on predictive understanding of seismicity. He introduced concepts of non-linear science to solid earth geophysics, considering the lithosphere as a hierarchical non-linear system. Later on he extended his research to a wider class of non-linear complex systems in nature and society. Keilis-Borok and his school made a major breakthrough in the study of the most important and least understood feature of non-linear systems, persistent self-organization leading to abrupt overall changes. In different contexts those changes are called critical transitions, extreme events, bifurcations, disasters, catastrophes, and crises. He found basic regularities in development of critical phenomena and launched successful experiments in their advance predictions. This was done first for catastrophic earthquakes worldwide; later—for socio-economic phenomena, such as electoral change of a governing party, economic recessions, surges of unemployment, and crime waves. In collaboration with disaster management teams, he extended this work to optimization of disasters preparedness.

Fundamental discoveries:

1. Critical transitions in hierarchical non-linear systems. Keilis-Borok discovered a set of premonitory patterns of the system's dynamics preceding critical transitions. These patterns are reminiscent of the asymptotic behavior of a statistical physics system near the

11

critical point. However, unlike in statistical physics, Keilis-Borok ad-

Volodya Keilis-Borok (left) and Alexander Soloviev (right)

dressed not the equilibrium state, but the growing non-equilibrium, culminated by a critical transition.

2. Long-range correlations in seismicity, established as a major factor in generation of strong earthquakes.

3. Colliding cascade model of hierarchical systems, capturing the interaction between direct cascades of loading and inverse cascades of failures. This model exhibits complex dynamics of hierarchical systems, including (for the first time) the major premonitory patterns.

4. "Geometric" instability of tectonic fault networks, concentrated in the "nodes"—mosaic structures around fault intersections where strong earthquakes nucleate. Such nodes have been identified

worldwide, indicating previously unknown areas where strong earthquakes are possible. In the areas with low background seismicity, such nodes indicate the possibility of destructive creep.

5. Self-adapting earthquake prediction algorithms, put to unprecedented test by advance predictions worldwide.

6. Socio-economic predictions, including elections, recessions, unemployment surges, and crime waves.

7. Optimization of disaster preparedness in response to earthquake prediction, using the methods of mathematical economics and theory of optimal control.

8. Determination of the blocks-and-fault structure of the lithosphere, based on the integration of geological and geomorphological data. Numerous previously unknown active faults and areas where strong earthquakes might nucleate were successfully identified by means of this approach. The results are confirmed by data analysis in 11 regions worldwide.

9. Seismological inversion: non-uniqueness and its reduction. Major applications include recognition of underground nuclear explosions and oil exploration.

10. Theory of seismic surface waves, based on the mathematical theory of operators.

Practical importance:

Catastrophic earthquakes and other extreme events addressed in Keilis-Borok's studies pose commonly recognized unacceptable threats to the global village. Their understanding and prediction is pivotal for disasters reduction and control. Keilis-Borok and his school extended their fundamental studies to other applications, often "hot" and controversial: geological instability of megacities; seismic zoning and safety of nuclear power plants; political and socio-economic instabilities; and detection of underground nuclear explosions.

Impact and projected influence:

Keilis-Borok and his school revolutionized disaster prediction science. His integrated approach reinstated earthquake prediction as the frontier problem of geosciences. So far, Keilis-Borok's is the only group conducting real-time algorithmic prediction of individual strong earthquakes in numerous regions worldwide. Their results have enhanced the current capability for damage reduction and paved the way for deeper predictive understanding of geodynamics. Projected influence of Keilis-Borok's results extends to creating "universal" theory of extreme events in hierarchical complex systems. Promising pilot results include: (i) Thermodynamics (phase transitions in cluster dynamics); (ii) Hydrodynamics (generation of eddies by a jet of fluid); (iii) Precursory transformation of scaling in natural and man-made systems.

Teaching:

Keilis-Borok founded and directed biennial International Workshops on Non-Linear Dynamics and Earthquake Prediction at the Abdus Salam International Center for Theoretical Physics, Trieste, Italy. He included public policy aspects of disaster prediction into the curriculum of the EU International Graduate School for Comparative Public Policy Analysis, Luxemburg. The principal feature of his teaching work was "learning by doing"—an effective tool for knowledge transfer.

Style:

Keilis-Borok's trademark is the seemingly impossible connection between different fields of research and/or different groups of experts. He broke the barriers between high theory, numerical modeling, and data analysis. Collaborations that he organized include top experts from mathematics, physics, economics, and social sciences, working together with experts from law enforcement, disaster management, environment protection, and the government. He had founded a unique institute, where "pure" mathematicians worked jointly with geophysicists and geologists, including world-famous mathematicians, such as I. Gelfand, L. Kantorovich, Ya. Sinai, Yu. Osipov and their schools, and geoscientists, such as F. Press, L. Knopoff, C. Allègre, and D. Rundkvist. At the peak of the Cold War he made bold contributions to the détente, reaching understanding with the international experts at the nuclear test ban negotiations. He founded the famous International Symposia on Mathematical Geophysics, which brought together leading mathematicians and geoscientists from the opposite sides of the Iron Curtain.

His distinctive style is illustrated by the fact that he was elected into the US National Academy of Sciences 17 years earlier than into the Academy of Sciences of the USSR, his home country. His first major international election, into the American Academy of Arts and Sciences, occurred simultaneously with the elections of A. Sakharov, A. Solzhenitsyn and L. Kantorovich. He occupied several top international positions in his field, including the President of the International Union of Geodesy and Geophysics, and achieved highly prestigious international honors, including Richardson Medal for Achievements in Non-Linear Dynamics.

V.I.Keilis-Borok's Career

Alexander A. Soloviev, Director, MITPAN:

Education

In 1943 Vladimir Keilis-Borok graduated from the Department of Geology of the Moscow Geological Exploration Institute and started his scientific career as a post graduate student at the Geophysical Institute, the USSR Academy of Sciences (now – the O. Yu. Schmidt Institute of the Physics of the Earth, the Russian Academy of Sciences). He was lucky to have a famous Russian mathematician Nickolai Luzin as a scientific supervisor. Luzin, an outstanding representative of the Russian mathematical school that is famous for the traditional interest of "pure" mathematicians to the applied problems, imparted to Keilis-Borok a deep interest in application of modern mathematical and computational methods to solving actual problems of geology and geophysics.

For more than 20 years Keilis-Borok studied the problems of wave seismology. In 1948 he received his Ph. D. degree and in 1953 – Doctor of Science (there are two advanced degrees in Russia). He was 32 and one of the youngest among geophysicists who had Doctor of Science degree (In the USSR and Russia scientists receive usually this degree when they are over 40). His work on seismic waves resulted in the development of a new theory of seismic surface waves based on the spectral theory of operators.

Analysis of Seismic Waves

Among the many applications of this work, a prominent role belongs to the detection of underground nuclear explosions by analysis of surface waves. This possibility, discovered simultaneously by Frank Press in the USA and Vladimir Keilis-Borok in the Soviet Union, provided the turning point on the international technical discussions on nuclear test ban treaty (Geneva, 1959-1961). Keilis-Borok was among the very few Soviet experts invited to these negotiations. In Geneva, he met distinguished American scientists, including Frank Press, and his meetings with Keilis-Borok initiated their fruitful scientific collaboration and friendship.

Computational Seismology

Keilis-Borok had formulated a general view on the inverse problems of seismology and had given them an exact form. He initiated pure mathematical studies of uniqueness and stability for these problems. These studies resulted in ideas, which got a concentrated expression in one of his most important papers "Seismology and Logics" published in 1964 (Keilis-Borok, V.I. Seismology and logic // Research in Geophysics. S.l., 1964. Vol. 2: Solid Earth and Interface Phenomena. The M.I.T. Press. P.61-79).

Keilis-Borok tackled the main problem that arose in seismology at that time: the problem of processing and interpretation of huge flows of seismological information coming from the emerging global network of seismic stations. He saw only one solution of this problem: standardization and formalization of the work of seismologists. At that time this approach started a revolution in seismology.

Keilis-Borok was the first among the Soviet scientists who demonstrated the necessity of implementation of computers in geophysics and indicated the most effective ways of their usage. At that time a new basic branch of geophysics—computational seismology—was being formed, and Keilis-Borok became one of its founders. As one of the keystones in this process he created the International Committee for Geophysical Theory and Computers (now—IUGG Committee on Mathematical Geophysics), an organization that brought together many outstanding geophysicists from all over the world.

Keilis-Borok was the Founding Chairman of the Committee and headed it from the first meeting in 1964 until 1979. At the same time he established the Department of Computational Geophysics at the Institute of the Physics of the Earth.

As the head of this Department, Keilis-Borok devoted his attention to organizing scientific teams oriented on solving specific problems. He picked the best scientists for these teams, coming from all over the Soviet Union and from abroad. Keilis-Borok personally participated in all stages of problem solving, drilling down into the details. His leadership style was very effective: each member of the team acted in perfect synergy to achieve a common goal.

Keilis-Borok became one of the world leaders in geophysics. His contributions had been recognized through his memberships in the American Academy of Arts and Sciences (AAAS, 1969) and the U.S. National Academy of Sciences (NAS, 1971). His election into AAAS recognized not only his scientific achievements, but his insight into the poetry of Boris Pasternak, one of the best Russian poets of the twentieth century. Keilis-Borok had memorized many Pasternak's poems and recited his poetry in appropriate cases, using these quotations freely and effectively to express his feelings and illustrate his point. Poetry quotations for all occasions were among his distinguishing features. He also had a deep understanding of art. He was a close friend of a famous Russian painter Yuri Vasiliev and a poet Yevgeny Yevtushenko, and others.

Keilis-Borok initiated development of a new methodology for *optimization of disasters' preparedness*: measures undertaken in response to predictions with a limited accuracy. One of the key ideas of this methodology was to estimate an average economic effect of antiseismic measures. These studies were initiated in collaboration with Leonid Kantorovich, an outstanding mathematician and economist, Nobel Prize laureate in economics. The approach they developed was applied in 1968-69 for estimating antiseismic measures for Baikal-Amur Transsiberian Railway.

Defining Earthquake-Prone Nodes

In early 1970s Keilis-Borok took on a problem of defining earth-quake-prone areas, in collaboration with Elizaveta Ranzman, a professor of geomorphology, and with a famous mathematician Israel Gelfand, whose group who developed the methodology of pattern recognition of infrequent events. The main idea was to consider "nodes"—mosaic structures around fault intersections where instability is concentrated and strong earthquakes can potentially nucleate. Such nodes were analyzed by pattern recognition methods to identify those of them where strong earthquakes were truly possible.

The first papers, focused on Central Asia, were published in 1972. After that the approach was applied to many areas worldwide. The study for California and Nevada was published in 1976 in collaboration with Frank Press and another outstanding American geophysicist Leon Knopoff. Remarkably, the epicenters of all 15 strong earthquakes that occurred in this region since 1976 were within the earthquake-prone nodes identified in this study.

Earthquake Predictions

Next, Keilis-Borok focused on developing a method for intermediate-term earthquake prediction. He formulated the necessary conditions for earthquake precursors, focusing on formalization and usage of the data that would be available and uniform in different seismically active regions. It explains the choice of precursors based on seismicity data—the catalogs of earthquakes. The first precursor that was formally determined through this work was "Pattern Σ", introduced in 1964 and comprising the premonitory increase in activity of the background seismicity. After that, a precursor termed as "Burst of aftershocks" was formulated and formalized, enabling the use of catalogs where magnitudes of small and medium earthquakes were not determined. This precursor was used for one of the first successful predictions—the prediction of Irpinia earthquake in Italy (1980).

Analysis of solitary precursors showed that their independent use cannot be a basis for reliable earthquake prediction. Using the concept of the lithosphere as a nonlinear dynamical complex system with strong earthquakes as extreme events in it, Keilis-Borok deduced that successful predictions should utilize a complex of precursors. This idea served as a basis for the generation of such complex earthquake prediction algorithms, including algorithm CN, developed on the basis of the seismicity data for California and Nevada, and algorithm M8, designed for prediction of the strongest (with magnitude $M \geq$ 8.0) earthquakes worldwide. These algorithms were used for the prediction of Loma Prieta earthquake in California (1989).

The prediction of Loma Prieta earthquake, made in advance, attracted the attention of Presidents Ronald Reagan and Mikhail Gorbachev and influenced the decision to create the International Institute of Earthquake Prediction Theory and Mathematical Geophysics, Academy of Sciences of the USSR (MITPAN RAN). This Institute, established on January 1st, 1990, was formed on the basis of the Department of Computational Geophysics of the Schmidt Institute of the Physics of the Earth. Keilis-Borok was its Founding Director until 1998.

In 1987, in recognition of his contribution to geophysics, Keilis-Borok was elected the President of the International Union of Geodesy and Geophysics. In December of the same year he was elected a full member of the Academy of Sciences of the USSR—the top recognition for a scientist in Russia.

In 1992 Keilis-Borok initiated a Russian-American experiment aimed at a real-time intermediate-term prediction of the strongest ($M \geq 8.0$) earthquakes on a global scale using the M8 algorithm. 14 out of 19 earthquakes have been successfully predicted within the framework of this experiment. The predicted earthquakes include the Chile earthquake (February 27th, 2010, $M = 8.8$) and the Japan earthquake (March 11th, 2011, $M = 9.0$). Alarms declared by the algorithm covered about 30% of the total time-space area. Statistical significance of the predictions exceeded 99%. The results of the experiment gave nontrivial statistical justification of the possibility of the intermediate-term earthquake prediction. These results also confirmed the important postulate of the M8 algorithm that the strongest earthquakes originate in the areas with linear size about 1500 km.

Basing on developing these earthquake prediction algorithms Keilis-Borok has formulated the following steps of a general procedure that, in principle, could be applied to developing prediction algorithms for other extreme events:

1. Choosing prediction targets. In the case of earthquakes it means the choice of the threshold magnitude for the target earthquakes.

2. Choosing the background fields where we hope to detect precursors. Prediction of strong earthquakes is based on seismicity patterns in lower magnitude range, but any potentially relevant field can be considered.

3. Formulation of a hypothetical prediction algorithm. That is done by the *pattern recognition of rare events*—the methodology developed by the school of I. Gelfand for studying rare events of highly complex origin.

4. Validation of prediction algorithm by prediction in advance.

Keilis-Borok persistently adhered to the holistic approach in the development of prediction algorithms. This can be explained as follows. Natural science had for many centuries regarded the Universe as a completely predictable machine. As Pierre Simon de Laplace wrote in 1776, "…if we knew exactly the laws of nature and the situation of the universe at the initial moment, we could predict exactly the situation of the same universe at a succeeding moment." However, at the turn of the 20th century (1905) Jules Henry Poincare discovered, that "… this is not always so. It may happen that small differences in the initial conditions will produce very great ones in the final phenomena. Prediction becomes impossible". This instability of initial conditions is indeed a definitive attribute of complex systems. Nonetheless, through the robust integral description of such systems, it is possible to discover their regular behavior patterns transcending the inherent complexity. For that reason studying complexity requires the holistic approach that proceeds from the whole to details, as opposed to the reductionism approach that proceeds from details to the whole.

Keilis-Borok formulated four paradigms that provide a guidance for the search for premonitory patterns in the earthquake prediction.

Paradigm 1: Basic types of premonitory patterns. As a target earthquake draws near, the background seismic activity becomes more intense and clustered in space–time, while the correlation range in space increases and size distribution (scaling relation) shifts in favor of relatively stronger events.

Paradigm 2: Large size of precursor manifestation area. Generation of a target earthquake is not localized in its vicinity. This may be explained by several mechanisms that range from micro-fluctuations of large scale tectonic movements to impact of migrating fluids.

Paradigm 3: Similarity. Quantitative definition of prediction algorithms is self-adjusting to regional conditions. For example, earthquake prediction algorithms developed for seismicity of California demonstrate their applicability to other active regions, with the magnitude of the target events varying from 3.0 to 6.6, for starquakes, and, at the other end of the spectrum, for fracturing in engineering constructions and laboratory samples. The energy of a target event in these applications ranges from ergs (micro-fracture) to 10^{26} ergs (major earthquake), and even to 10^{41} ergs (starquake).

Paradigm 4. Dual nature of premonitory patterns. The premonitory patterns are "universal", common for hierarchical complex systems of different origin. They can be reproduced in the models of dynamical clustering, branching diffusion, percolation, direct, inverse, and colliding cascades, as well as in certain system-specific models.

Keilis-Borok and his group continued perfecting their algorithms, aiming to achieve shorter-term predictions and to improve their accuracy. One of the last earthquake prediction algorithms developed by Keilis-Borok's group is "Reverse Tracing of Precursors" (RTP). The algorithm is aimed at predictions about 9 months in advance, much shorter than by the M8 algorithm. As its name suggests, RTP traces precursors in the reverse order of their formation. First it identifies "candidates" for short-term precursors—long, rapidly formed chains of earthquakes in the background seismicity. Such chains reflect an increase in the earthquake correlation range. Next, each chain is examined to determine whether there have been any preceding intermediate-term precursors in its vicinity within the previous five years.

If yes, the chain triggers an alarm.

Since 2003, the RTP algorithm has been tested by predicting future earthquakes in five regions of the world (California and adjacent regions; Central and Northern Italy with adjacent regions; Eastern Mediterranean; Northern Pacific, Japan and adjacent regions). Five out of seven target earthquakes have been predicted between 2003 and 2012 (captured by alarms) including the San Simeon earthquake in Central California (December 22nd, 2003, $M = 6.5$), and two were missed. Out of 19 alarms, five were correct and fourteen false, two of the latter being near misses occurring close to the alarm areas. The data are still insufficient for rigorous estimation of statistical significance.

Socio-Economic Predictions

Accepting the conception of the universality of extreme event precursors, Keilis-Borok applied the approaches developed in his work on earthquakes to socio-economic predictions. The first study in this direction was conducted in 1980-81 in collaboration with Professor Allan Lichtman (USA). Together, they developed an algorithm for prediction of the outcome of the Presidential elections in the U.S. This algorithm was based on the fact that the actual electoral decision was whether the incumbent party would win or lose, rather than whether the Republicans or Democrats would win. Prediction algorithm was developed by pattern recognition analysis of the data on 31 past elections, from 1860 (the election of Abraham Lincoln) to 1980 (the election of Ronald Reagan). All eight Presidential elections after the publication of the algorithm have been predicted correctly. That includes Al Gore's victory by popular vote in 2000, which was reversed by the electorate vote: a turn that happened only 3 times in history. Keilis-Borok said that one of the reasons for Bill Clinton's decision to run as a candidate for the Democrats in 1992 elections was the prediction announced by A. Lichtman that the challenger party (Democrats in that election) would win.

During the last 15 years Keilis-Borok worked on development of algorithms for prediction of extreme events in socio-economic systems: economic recessions (their onset and termination); surges of unemployment; and surges of crime. For surges of unemployment in the U.S., advance predictions have been in progress since 1999. Two recent episodes (June 2000 and December 2007) have been predicted correctly, without failures or false alarms.

He was a real pioneer who inspired us so much, and a kind, compassionate person. I owe him tremendously.

Alexander A. Soloviev

Curriculum Vitae

VLADIMIR I. KEILIS-BOROK

Institute of Geophysics and Planetary Physics
University of California
Los Angeles, California 90095-1567
phone: (310) 206-5667/ 825-1885
fax: (310) 206-3051
e-mail: vkb@ess.ucla.edu

EXPERIENCE

1999-2013   Professor-in-Residence, Institute of Geophysics and Planetary Physics, University of California, Los Angeles (half time)

1998-2013   Research group leader, International Institute for Earthquake Prediction Theory and Mathematical Geophysics (MITPAN), Russian Academy of Sciences (half time)

1985-2013   Founder and co-Director, Research program and Workshop on non-linear dynamics and earthquake prediction, International Center for Theoretical Physics, Trieste.

1958-2002   Organizer of many international meetings and symposia, including study week on Basic Science for Survival and Sustainable Development and Discussion on contribution of basic science to fighting terrorism, in the Pontifical Academy of Sciences, Vatican

1969-1999   Visiting Professor: UCLA, Purdue University, MIT, CIT, Harvard University, Universities of Trieste and

Rome (La Sapienza), Institute of Earth Physics (Paris), and others.

1989-1998 Founder and Director, MITPAN, Russia

1948-1989 Institute of the Physics of the Earth, Academy of Sciences, USSR. Last position held – Founder and Chairman, Department of Computational Geophysics, 1970-1989

HONORS

Since 1999 Academia Europaea, UK

Since 1994 Pontifical Academy of Sciences, Vatican (member of the Council since 1996)

Since 1992 Austrian Academy of Sciences, Austria

Since 1989 Royal Astronomical Society, UK

Since 1988 Russian Academy of Sciences, Russia

Since 1971 National Academy of Sciences, USA

Since 1969 American Academy of Arts and Sciences, USA

1998 Richardson medal for achievements in non-linear dynamics

1998 Regents Professor, University of California, Los Angeles, USA

1995 Doctor Honoris Causa, Institut de Physique du Globe, Paris, France

1978,1979 Fairchild Distinguished Scholar, California Institute of Technology, USA

MEMBERSHIP IN SCIENTIFIC ORGANIZATIONS

1997-2013 Member, Russian Academy of Sciences Committee for International Security and Disarmament

1993-1999　　Member, Council of the Russian Foundation for Basic Research.

1994-1997　　Member, International Working Group on geological safety of the nuclear waste depositories.

1992-1997　　Member, Scientific Committee, EU International Association for Support of Basic Research in the Countries of the Former Soviet Union.

1987-1991　　President, International Union of Geodesy and Geophysics

1990-1991　　Member of the Union's Scientific Committee for International Decade for Natural Disasters Reduction.

1988-1991　　Board Member, International Council of Scientific Unions;

1964-1979　　Founder and Chairman, International Committee for Geophysical Theory and Computers, later renamed Committee for Mathematical Geophysics

1962　　　　 Expert, Technical meetings on the nuclear test ban treaty

EDITORIAL ACTIVITIES

1966-2013　　Founder and chief co-editor, Series: Computational Seismology and Geodynamics, published in Russia and USA

Member of other editorial boards.

RECENT AWARDS

2000-2003　　"Understanding and Prediction of Critical Transitions in Complex Systems. The 21st Century Collaborative Activity Award for Studying Complex Systems. McDonnell

Foundation. Principal Investigator.

1985-2013 "Non-linear dynamics and earthquake prediction". International Centre for Theoretical Physics, Trieste. Research leader

1998 – 2000 "Application of Dynamic Systems to Earthquake Prediction," NSF, Co-P.I.

1992 - 1999 "Intermediate - term earthquake prediction." Grants from the International Council of Scientific Union, NAS, and other agencies, Chairman

1993-1999 "Multiple fracturing of solids," Co-P.I., grant from the European Union.

1997-1999 "Development of intercomputer network for geophysical studies in F.S.U.," grant from the European Union, Co-P.I.

1997 - 1999 "Application of R&D in military aviation systems to problems of mitigation of damage from the earthquakes," Research leader, grant from the International Science and Technology Center.

1994 - 1998 "Non-linear dynamics of solid Earth and its applications," (French-Russian project). Co-chairman, grant from the French National Research Council.

1995 – 1997 "Conversion of R&D in missile navigation to mathematical problems of ecology and natural hazards," Research leader, grant from the International Science and Technology Center.

1993-1996 "Advanced Training in seismic risk evaluation," Project leader, grant from International Reinsurance Company MAPFRE (Spain).

1992-1995 "Advanced studies in theoretical geophysics," Research leader, grants 1998 from Schlumberger Foundation.

1994-1995 "Chaos and Critical Phenomena in the Earth's Lithosphere," P.I., grant from the Soros Foundation.

<u>MAJOR FINDINGS</u>

Prediction of critical phenomena in hierarchical non-linear dissipative systems with applications to prediction of earthquakes and socioeconomic crises

1. Integration of mathematical modeling and data analysis
- Development of colliding cascade models for prediction of critical phenomena
- Introduction of pattern recognition of infrequent events into analysis of complex systems
2. Development of and test of algorithms for intermediate earthquake prediction
3. Development of and test of algorithms for socioeconomic predictions of the:
- Outcome of American Presidential and midterm Senatorial elections
- US economic recessions
- Surges of unemployment in Western Europe and USA
- Crime waves in mega cities

Tectonic fault network

1. Long-range interactions within the tectonic fault network
2. Mechanisms of instability, particularly rock-fluid interaction
3. Integral measures of instability
4. Models of dynamics of the network
5. Recognition of structures where earthquakes and destructive creep nucleate

Seismic risk

1. Probabilistic estimates of seismic risk in terms of damage to population and economy (particularly for mega cities)
2. Methods for optimization of risk reduction and earthquake preparedness

Seismic waves

1. Establishment of non-uniqueness of inversion and methods to overcome it
2. Introduction of operators' theory into theory of surface waves.
3. Introduction of the surface waves (contrary to the direction of the first arrivals only) into identification of underground nuclear explosions.

ONGOING RESEARCH

- critical transitions in hierarchical chaotic systems
- non-linear dynamics and critical phenomena of lithosphere
- dynamics of seismicity
- earthquake prediction
- socio-economic predictions

PUBLICATIONS

Approximately 420 publications in peer-reviewed journals. Partial list available at http://www.mitp.ru

V. I. KEILIS-BOROK'S LIFE

1921-2013

"He only earns his Freedom and Existence,
Who's forced to win them freshly every day."

Goethe, *Faust.*

Volodya, the Name

Volodya is the "short", informal form of Vladimir—an old Russian name that literally translates as "Own the World". Some of the legendary Russian princes and kings carried this name. An old city named Vladimir is a part of the "Golden Ring of Russia". At the same time, based on some phonetic similarities (Velvel, Wolfer), this name was also adopted by Russian Jews, who considered it their own.

In the Russian language this name is never used in its official form, but always derivatized in different ways to reflect the relationships with different people. Thus, Volodya Keilis-Borok became known to different people by different derivatives of his name. His parents and older relatives abbreviated this name as Vova, the nickname that stayed on through his childhood. He became known as Volodya somewhere after his student years. When he became a professor at a very young age of 33, his colleagues started calling him more and more by his respectful formal name, Vladimir Isaakovich. When he started to travel abroad, it was of course impossible for foreigners to use this double name, so he started introducing himself as Volodya again, and as a result the majority of people who knew him called him this way. He also preferred to use this name at home, and even his granddaughter and great-grandchildren called him Volodya.

In this book these names are used interchangeably, based on the point of view and the period of his life.

Early Life

Anna Kashina, granddaughter:

Volodya was born in Moscow in 1921, only three years after the October Communist Revolution in 1917. His father, Isaak Moiseevich Keilis, was a jeweler and a member of the local Jewish community. His mother, Ksenia Ruvimovna Borok, also a Jew, came to Moscow from Lithuania to participate in rebuilding of the newly created Soviet Union. She belonged to the Left Menshevik party. After Bolsheviks took over, she soon realized that her activities within her party would only get her in trouble, so she abandoned her political undertakings and settled for the married life.

Volodya with his parents

Volodya with his father

Volodya was an only child. He told us very little about his early years. His father spent several years in and out of prison, during the beginning of Stalin's regime—fortunately, before the worst of it in 1937, which was why he survived. Some of Volodya's uncles and other relatives were "repressed" and died or disappeared without a trace. His mother managed to maintain a job during these difficult times, working as a secretary to the famous polar investigator and geophysicist O. Yu. Schmidt. She was always willing to help those in need. Once, she met an educated German woman who was left homeless and without means of survival after her husband had been repressed. Since the woman would not accept any charity, Volodya's mother hired her as a governess for little Vova, taking the woman into her household. As a result, Volodya grew up speaking German. Until certain age he knew it even better than Russian, since his parents spoke Yiddish at home.

He continued to think of German as his first language until World War II, when, in 1941, Germany attacked Russia. Volodya told me that on that day he instantly forgot every word of German, and never spoke it since. He claimed not to understand it either, and only later in life did he sometimes admit vaguely understanding some of the German words.

At some point later, Volodya decided to learn English. Since he had learned German early on just by speaking it, he never believed in formal language training and thought that the best way to learn would be to pick up a book and read. He did just that, reading all the Eng-

Volodya with his mother

lish-language literature he could lay his hands on, using a dictionary to translate each word. Remarkably, it worked. Volodya spoke charming idiomatic English—perhaps with a special Russian flavor that made it seem even more alluring. One thing he never learned, though, was the correct pronunciation. He pronounced the words the way they were spelled, often making it difficult to understand him. His cousin Inna remembers asking him once: "Why don't you take the time to learn proper pronunciation?" Volodya replied: "I can pronounce correctly if I focus on it, but this effort take away from my ability to formulate my thoughts." Later in life, after traveling abroad for many years, he polished it up enough not to make it a handicap in a conversation, but I will always remember how my English teacher absolutely forbade him to speak English in my presence for the fear of spoiling my training in what she considered to be the proper English accent.

One of the earliest episodes in his life he told me about: he was about six years old and lived with his family in the center of Moscow, next to a big library. One day, he went out by himself and found his way into the library, where he picked up a novel by Turgenev and settled to read. He was so absorbed in the book that he did not notice how the day passed and it became dark. After he finished reading it took him a while to come back to reality and realize how late it was. He ran home and found his mother crying and all the neighbors searching for him. His mother did not scold him, but he felt so ashamed. This memory of the way he got so absorbed, how amazed he was at Turgenev's prose, how ashamed of causing his mother so much worry, stayed with him for many years.

Крым. Артек. Пионеры у балюстрады.

His mother used his ability to get absorbed in reading to another end. During those hungry times, everyone tried to feed their children as much as they could, and Volodya was not a big eater. When he was reading a book, however, he wasn't paying attention, and so his mother could put food in front of him and he would eat it without thinking. He did it later in life too, eating "automatically" and very fast when he was preoccupied, and refusing food when he was aware of it. He always said that food numbed his brain and made him sleepy, so he tried to control how much he ate when he wanted to stay alert, and ate bread on purpose if he wanted to sleep or stop worrying.

He was always the top student in his class. In his memory, he never spent time studying or doing homework. Knowledge came naturally, without conscious efforts. He was so good that during his "pioneer" years (3rd to 8th grade) he earned the high honor of going to the Artek summer camp in Crimea, the place that collected the best students from the entire Soviet Union. It was a wondrous place for a child from Moscow, with the warm Black Sea, the palms, the fruits, the beautiful scenery. Volodya never spoke of it to me, but I found some postcards he wrote to his parents when he was there. Among other things, these postcards show how big of a worrier he was, even at that age.

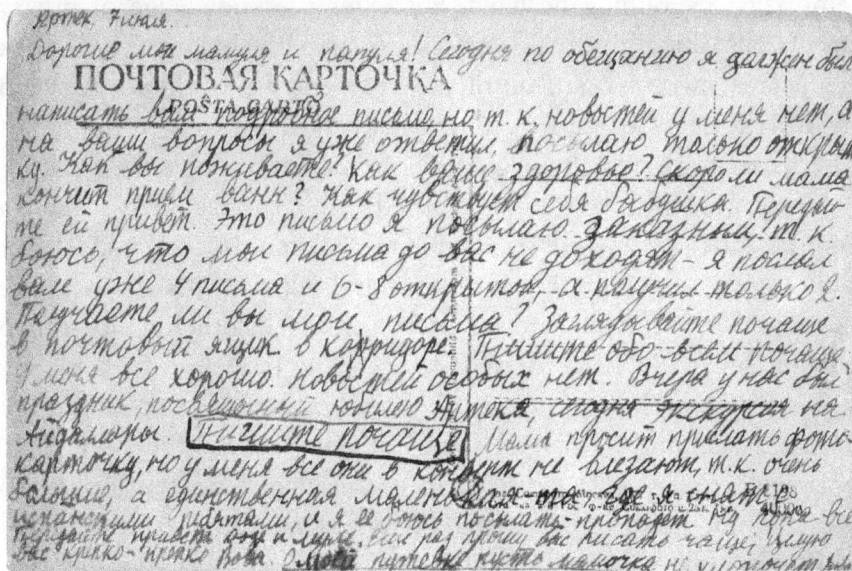

A postcard Volodya sent from the Artek summer camp to his parents.

<u>Front (previous page):</u> *"This is our uniform. If it is very hot we wear tank tops instead of shirts."*

<u>Back:</u> *"Artek, July 7, Dear mom and dad! Today, as promised, I was supposed to write you a detailed letter, but since I don't have any news and I already answered your questions, I am sending you only a postcard. How are you? How is your health? How soon will mama finish her bath therapy? How is grandma feeling? Say hello to her. I am sending this letter via special delivery since I am worried you are not receiving my letters. I already sent you 4 letters and 6-8 postcards, but received only 2. Are you receiving my letters? You should check the mailbox in the hallway more often. Write to me more often about everything. I am fine. No special news. Yesterday we celebrated Artek's anniversary, today we are going on a tour of Aidalloras. Write more often. Mama asked to send photos, but they don't fit into the envelope because they are too big, the only small one is where I am standing with the Spanish kids and I am afraid to send it—it will be lost. This seems to be all. Say hi to Dodi and Mulya. I am asking you again to write more often. Kisses to everyone. Vova. Ask mom not to be concerned with my travel arrangements. Vova."*

He loved classical literature, and especially poetry, instantly memorizing everything he liked. His extensive knowledge of poetry exceeded anything imaginable, at least for me. Pushkin and Pasternak became his favorites, and until the very end he could recite them much better than any of us. Among his very last words, in the fall of 2013, he recited to me the beginning of Pushkin's "Eugeny Onegin."

He always considered himself gifted with a special ability to talk, a talent to convince anyone of anything. He often mocked himself for it, but he was also secretly proud of it and felt that this ability, more than anything else, facilitated his entire career. His other ability was to maintain several lines of thought at the same time and to divide his attention without losing threads of several activities. At school he sat in classes thinking of several things at once and at the same time managing to keep full attention on the teacher. Since he looked so distracted, the teachers often called him and asked him to repeat everything that was just said. He always did, without hesitation, and almost word to word. Eventually the teachers gave up, acknowledging his superiority. His classmates were proud of him and often showed off his ability to instantly come up with an eloquent and efficient speech on nearly any topic.

Later on, he used this ability to help me prepare for my school exams in social sciences, which at those times meant the history, theory, and practice of Communism. I could not possibly get the logic of these disciplines and Volodya always came to my aid, instantly coming up with answers to any question in the book. I wrote them down and later did my best to memorize what he said; this was the only way I could pass these disciplines with decent grades.

Overall, his ability to talk, maintain his attention on several things, formulate things so efficiently and beautifully, all came from the same root: his talent to instantly enfold a complex problem and translate it into a few words everyone could understand. This talent helped him immensely in his work, where he developed a special ability to organize and lead unique teams of scientists from different areas and ensure that they all spoke a common language. Such teams were instrumental in many of his scientific achievements.

In his own words, however, being so eloquent did not always serve him well. As a child, he often spoke without being aware of the consequences, making jokes that could be perceived as dangerous at the times of Stalin's repressions. His relatives often said that Volodya's talking would be the death of him, which fortunately turned out not to be the case. He often felt embarrassed after he talked too frankly, or felt keenly the embarrassment of others, and over time he developed a habit to control his words—even though by his own admission, he did not always succeed. One of the Communist slogans at those times was "Stop idle talk" ("Ne boltai"), and Volodya often repeated these words to himself, and even posted them on his office wall at some point.

He recalled two episodes when he was a student. Once, he and his friend were chatting on a street corner and, to illustrate some point he could not remember, Volodya took out a paper banknote with the portrait of Lenin and used a pencil to extend Lenin's mustache and beard. If noticed, this would have led to Volodya's arrest and disappearance. But his friend, with a great presence of mind, took the banknote from Volodya's hand and erased the pencil drawings before anyone could see it. Volodya always felt this friend saved his life.

Another time, Volodya went to see a new movie that just came out in theatres. He loved movies and often said that watching movies helped him organize his thoughts, so he tried to watch every new release. But this particular one turned out to be a propaganda movie about Stalin. About halfway through Volodya felt he couldn't possibly take it any more and walked out, fully aware that this may be considered criminal disrespect. As he strode away from the theater, he kept listening, expecting the guards to chase and arrest him. Preparing for the questioning, he quickly made up a story. He would tell the guards that he had seen this movie eighteen times and today he came specifically to watch the particularly enlightening scene of Comrade Stalin walking in the garden. He never believed this obvious lie would work, but fortunately no one tried to arrest him and so he never had to put this story to the test. When he told this to me many years later,

I thought it was hilarious, but of course I had no idea what it was like to live in those times.

Family

Anna Kashina:

Volodya met his first wife, Galina Andreenva Ivanova (Galya) when he was still in college. They married around the start of the war, in 1941. As a student, Volodya was exempt from the army. Many of his classmates and friends joined, and he always felt ashamed for staying behind. He wanted to volunteer, but his mother told him this decision would kill her, and, reluctantly, he followed his family to evacuation. While he admits that this decision very likely saved his life, on another level he always regretted this.

He recalled an episode when he was in evacuation with his wife and mother. A group of soldiers were passing by and they stopped by the well to freshen up and chat with Volodya. They

Volodya and Galya

45

were still talking when Galya came out of the house and started shouting for Volodya to come home immediately. The soldiers laughed: "Who is she? Your mother?" Volodya felt at that moment that he would love to run away with them or die, not to bear this shame. He was very young then, barely twenty—by his own admission, not ready for a family at all.

Volodya and Ira in Crimea

Volodya and Ira in on a boat trip

Volodya and Ira on a picnic

In 1944 Volodya and Galya had a daughter, Ira (my mother). Volodya poured all his love into her. When, about ten years later, Volodya and Galya decided to divorce, Ira made a choice to stay with him, which Volodya strongly supported. She told me later that living with Galya would have meant an even, uneventful life, while with Volodya her life acquired so much more color, full of fun and wonder, not always smooth, but so fascinating that she never even considered any alternatives. She remembered the feeling how, when Volodya was leaving Galya, she wanted to be with him, and nowhere else. Even Galya's open resentment of this decision did not make my mother hesitate.

Raising a daughter in these times was very challenging for a single father. Volodya managed it admirably, but he always doubted himself. His mental picture of Ira was that of a brave, self-sacrificing child,

Volodya and Ira

Volodya and Ira

and he always felt he needed to do more to deserve her love and trust. He was even more overwhelmed when, at sixteen, she decided to maintain his Jewish family name, rather than settling for her mother's Russian last name, Ivanova. In Soviet Russia having a Jewish name meant a big disadvantage in college choice and job placement, but she never even considered doing otherwise.

Volodya and Ira spent a lot of time traveling. Many times they just took walking trips in the countryside and knocking on doors in villages to ask for shelter for the night. By the time I was old enough to go on such trips the times have changed—as well as our means, which enabled us now to travel in a more upscale way. I re-

Ira Keilis-Borok at 16

47

Volodya, Lucia, and Ira

Volodya and Lucia

member going on a village trip once, when I was about four, and we spent the night in a house sleeping on the floor with Volodya, my mother, and several other people.

Volodya often took Ira to soccer games, joined by his friends, A. S. Monin, V. Ya. Barlas, and others. It was not a regular outing for a little girl, but it was fun.

Volodya in Garm, Tadzhikistan,

On June 12, 1956, Volodya married his co-worker Ludmila Nikolaevna (Lucia) Malinovskaya. Lucia did not have children of her own. She also did not develop a close connection with Ira, who was resentful of this marriage. As a result, Volodya and Lucia maintained a relationship of mutual respect and friendship, but never formed deep emotional closeness.

Lucia spent a lot of her time helping her sister, Tanya, bring up a little daughter, Natasha, 5 years older than me.

48

Lucia in Caucasis mountains on a trip with Volodya

Lucia with the puppies from her dog, Ghella, an English cocker spaniel.

Volodya often took us on trips together. By that time he had a lot more capabilities of traveling to amazing places I would not have visited otherwise. Volodya's favorite trips were always to the mountains, where he felt so much at home—both through his background in geology and through the fact that he found the mountain scenery comforting and breathtaking at the same time. He always said that only in the mountains did he feel truly alive and free. Our two mountain trips that I remember the most: Dombai, a ski resort in Caucasis mountains (Lucia came along that time), and a seismological survey station in Garm, in Tadzhikistan, in the high mountains of Pamir. I was around 13. On that trip I was stunned not only by the mountains, but by the local lifestyle that seemed to have come straight out of *Thousand and One Nights*. People in that area lived in hand-made clay houses, women stayed separately from men and covered their faces in public, they all wore clothing that probably did not change much for several hundred years, and very few of them spoke Russian. It was one of the most exotic places I ever visited.

Volodya did his best to relay his love for the mountains to me. But while I did enjoy our trips, and the views, my love has always been in the forests. The place where our favorite scenery of mountains and forests met was Dilijan in Armenia, where we stayed in a composers' resort (no idea how Volodya managed to get an invitation) and took daily walks though beech forests on the mountain slopes. I was in high school then, and we spent a lot of time writing our novel "In the Name of the Queen", which was completed around 1983 during one of these trips and will be discussed later in this book.

In 1992 Lucia suffered a massive stroke that kept her in bed for a year, immobile and unable to speak. Volodya stayed by her side. She passed away on July 1, 1993.

***

Inna Klenitskaya, cousin:

Volodya was 6 years older than me. I was an only child and lived with my mother, while my father visited us from time to time. I first started interacting with him when I was 10 (at that time my mother and I came back from an exile; she had been sent to North Kazakhstan as the sister of "an enemy of the state", the victim of repressions). Because of this, having an older brother was especially important for me. Volodya and I were cousins, but we always considered ourselves as close as brother and sister. We had four other cousins: three girls and one boy. Volodya and I were always the closest. My mother and I lived in Leningrad, and Volodya and his parents lived in Moscow. But my mother and I often visited our Moscow aunts and Volodya and I saw each other.

My first childhood memories (before the exile): I am riding on Volodya's shoulders and he is telling me something very interesting. Next time we met already after the war, when my mother and I returned from evacuation. I lived in Moscow with Volodya's parents for a year (he was already married and lived separately), while my mother in Leningrad was restoring her rights to her room in our communal apartment. I was in 8th grade and attended a literature class in the House of Pioneers. Volodya spent a lot of time with me, took me around Moscow, talked to me about school and my literature class. When he learned that my teacher in that class was the writer Fraerman (the author of the famous young adult book "Wild Dog Dingo, or the Story of the First Love"), he smirked: "What kind of an indecent last name is that!" ("Fraerman" means "free man").

I met Volodya again during my visit to Moscow when I was in 10th grade. Once (I don't remember why) I told him I didn't like Pushkin. (In our school Pushkin's poetry was taught in such a boring way that it could evoke indifference at best.) Volodya was very surprised. "What do you mean, you don't like Pushkin?! Listen!" He stood up and recited "To the Poet" ("Poet, don't cherish the love of the people"...) I would never forget the way he spoke. Never in my life, before or after, did I hear such deep, emotional performance. Volodya finished the poem, and I remembered that he had thought of a new way to solve a task that everyone considered impossible. Everyone thought his way was wrong, and some laughed at such a

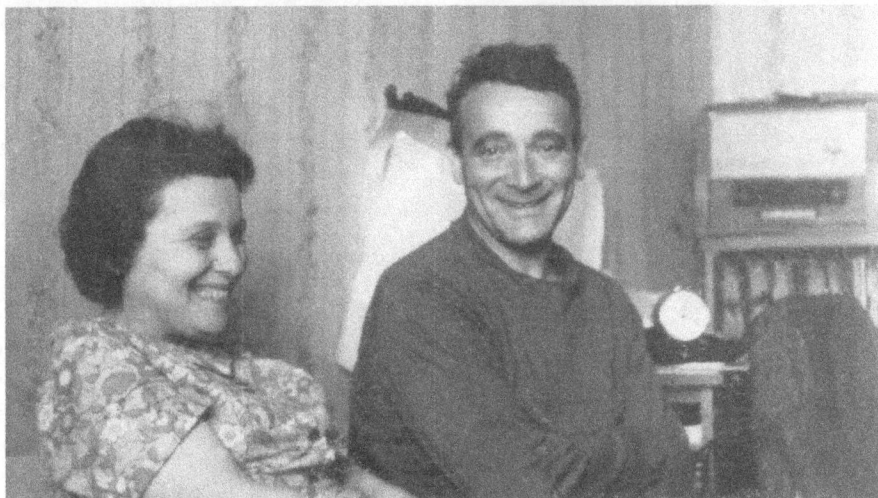

Inna and Volodya

51

self-assured student. (Later it turned out he was right.) From this I realized that Pushkin's poem was not only about a poet, but also about people like my brother (Volodya), who were true to their task, to their ideas, despite everything. "Not asking for rewards for your noble deed"... I re-read Pushkin, and he became my favorite poet. Much later, Volodya, by then thirty, recited to me his favorite lyrical verses from "Eugeny Onegin". He recited simply to share his admiration, his feelings that were so harmonious with the feelings of the poet. That time, he seemed especially emotional about the words "Is it true that I am nearing thirty?..."

I was always amazed about the way Volodya combined his love for science and his work with his love and deep understanding of poetry. When he was a student, this love for poetry brought him together with the future literary analyst and poetry expert, Vladimir Yakovlevich Barlas. Their friendship was truly amazing. Such unity of thought in everything, complete openness in every aspect of life, constant interactions. They even spent all their summers together, the

Volodya and V. Barlas

three of them (the third was Volodya's ten-year-old daughter, Ira.) When Vladimir Barlas dropped out of the graduate school at the Institute for Geological Prospecting to devote his time to literary criticism, my brother helped him to find freelance work translating geophysics papers, essential to provide a moderate income. Against general disapproval, Volodya supported his friend in this courageous decision. I remember the friends talking in the country house where he invited me in summer. Barlas sadly said that his articles were rarely published, he was not a member of the Writers Union, and more and more often he was thinking of how he was going to support himself when he grew old and retired. My brother immediately said: "Voloden'ka, I told you: we will manage together on my pension". (Soon, V. Barlas's articles became noticed, he published a book "In the Eyes of Poetry", and he was accepted into the prestigious Writers' Union. Too bad that later the two friends drifted apart...)

< *A.K.: Notably, V. Barlas's wife, E. Ranzman, was Volodya's key collaborator for many years, a lead scientist for the project on morphostructural analysis, which will be described in her article later in the book.* >

Volodya had an interesting reason for choosing not to study at the Moscow University, the best college in the country, and to go to the Institute for Geological Prospecting instead. He was in love with his classmate, who did not return his feelings. Before they graduated from high school, she communicated to him her intention to enter Moscow University and told Volodya that she did not want to have him as her classmate and would like him to choose another college. Volodya obliged.

< *A.K.: My mother and I heard of different reasons he chose his college over Moscow University, which had to do with advice he received when he was graduating from high school. We are not certain Inna's version is correct, but I am leaving it here for the sake of authenticity.* >

Volodya was very devoted to his daughter, and later to his granddaughter Anuta (Anna), as well as to all his relatives. (A lot is said by the fact that when Volodya divorced his first wife, his daughter wanted to stay with him. This wish was so strong that her mother, Volodya's first wife Galya, to her credit, accepted it without scandals, hysteria, or fighting).

When our cousin Shurik died of cancer, leaving a wife and four children, Volodya supported them, and later helped Shurik's oldest daughter to find a good job in Leningrad. (The family lived in Kronstadt). Volodya also helped me. My relationship with my first husband, Ilia, was strained. After finishing his obligatory work after college, Ilia returned to his parents in Moscow, and I—to my mother in Leningrad. I found myself without a job. Ilia also had trouble finding a job in his area. I lived with my mother and my daughter Ira on my mother's salary. When Volodya learned about that, he started sending me money, enough to lead a decent life. (When my husband found a job I naturally refused to receive money from Volodya anymore.)

A year later my husband and I got back together and I moved to Moscow. We lived in a very small apartment: me, with my husband and my daughter (and a year later also our newborn son Alexey), my mother-in-law (my father-in-law lived in the country house), two of my husband's sisters—one with her daughter, the other one with her husband—and a nanny, who had brought up all the children and became a full member of the family. My relationship with my husband did not go well, and two years later we divorced. When that happened, Volodya advised me to rent and apartment and hire a housekeeper (otherwise I would not be able to work), *and offered to pay for all of this!* (The problem eventually resolved in a different way: our three-story house was converted to an office building, all its inhabitants were relocated, and my children and I got a two-room apartment of our own.)

My brother was very attentive to my children, too. Once, when I was away, he came to our home and saw the following scene: my daughter Ira was standing with her head lowered, barely holding back tears, while her grandmother (my mother came to visit us from Leningrad) was scolding her for the mess in the kitchen. When the scolding was over, Volodya came up to Ira and said: "Let's go on a trip tomorrow!" My daughter was very happy (we all liked trips), and all next day (it was a weekend) Ira and "Uncle Vova" (that's what my children called him) had a wonderful time in a forest near Moscow.

My daughter still remembers that day. And when she became gravely ill and I was desperate, my brother went to the hospital with me and had a long conversation with the doctor...

Volodya was my support, a man I could always turn to for help and comfort... He was also a big supporter of my work and my new ideas in education.

He was very devoted to his work, but that part would be better told by his colleagues. Whenever he could not work, he became restless. I remember a funny verse his colleagues wrote during their trip to USA: "We have solved so many problems and scientific tasks, but nothing can satisfy this impossible man, Keilis-Borok!"

Institute of Physics of the Earth

Anna Kashina, Alexander A. Soloviev:

Immediately after high school (1938) Volodya entered Moscow Institute of Geological Prospecting (Moskovskii Geologo-Razvedochnyi Institut). He studied in the Department of Geophysics and graduated with honors as an engineer/geophysicist in 1943, to enter the graduate school at the Institute of Geophysics the USSR Academy of Sciences that later became the O. Yu. Schmidt Institute of Physics of the Earth (IPE). He stayed on at this Institute until the end of 1989.

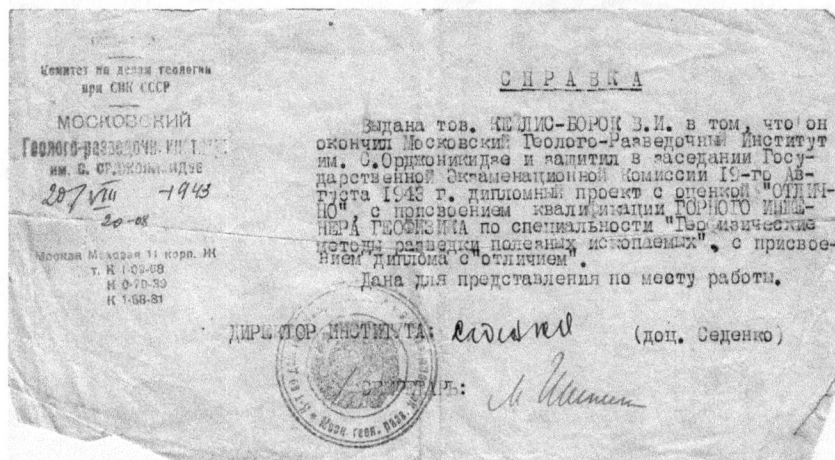

A certificate of college graduation, August 20, 1943

Volodya always wanted to be a mathematician, and he felt that he did not receive sufficient training in mathematics as an undergraduate, so he actively sought out the best supervision during his graduate training. N. N. Luzin, a legendary Russian mathematician, became his

ДИПЛОМ
КАНДИДАТА НАУК

МФМ № 00509

Москва 18 марта 1949 г.

Решением

гражданину

ПРИСУЖДЕНА УЧЕНАЯ СТЕПЕНЬ КАНДИДАТА
ФИЗИКО-МАТЕМАТИЧЕСКИХ НАУК

Ph.D. Diploma, March 18, 1949

ЗАЩИТА ДИССЕРТАЦИЙ НА СОИСКАНИЕ УЧЕНОЙ СТЕПЕНИ:

МОСКОВСКИЙ ТЕХНИЧЕСКИЙ ИНСТИТУТ РЫБНОЙ ПРОМЫШЛЕННОСТИ И ХОЗЯЙСТВА им. А. И. МИКОЯНА

9/IV—48 г., в 18 ч.:

1. На кандидата технических наук РЖАВСКОЙ Ф. М. на тему: «Изменение жира сельди при посоле».

2. На кандидата биологических наук НАУМОВЫМ В. М. на тему: «Изучение развития мурманской сельди».   678

МОСКОВСКИЙ ТЕКСТИЛЬНЫЙ ИНСТИТУТ

(Донская, 62).

8/IV—48 г., в 15 ч., на кандидата

ГЕОФИЗИЧЕСКИЙ ИНСТИТУТ АКАДЕМИИ НАУК СССР

(Пыжевский пер., 3)

14/IV—48 г., в 15 ч., на кандидата физико-математических наук КЕЙЛИС-БОРОК В. И. на тему: «Исследование колебаний свободной границы упругого полупространства под действием точечного источника».

ГОСУДАРСТВЕННЫЙ АСТРОНОМИЧЕСКИЙ ИНСТИТУТ им. ШТЕРНБЕРГА

(пер. Павлика Морозова, 5)

15/IV—48 г., в 11 ч., на кандидата физико-математических на-

Newspaper announcement about Volodya's Ph.D. Defense (top right)
on April 14, 1948

first teacher. Under his tutelage, Volodya began to pursue his ideas of applying "pure" mathematics of the famous Russian school to geology and geophysics.

Volodya received his Ph.D. in 1948 and stayed on at IPE, quickly rising in the ranks until, at the age of 33 he became a professor and the head of the newly formed Laboratory (later, in 1969, a Department containing several laboratories) of Computational Geophysics. The director of the Institute, M. A. Sadovsky, recognized Volodya's

ВЫСШАЯ АТТЕСТАЦИОННАЯ КОМИССИЯ
ПРИ МИНИСТЕРСТВЕ ВЫСШЕГО ОБРАЗОВАНИЯ
Москва, ул. Жданова, д. 11

ВЫПИСКА

из протокола № 19 от „23. октября 195 4 г.

(Подлинник протокола находится в делах Высшей аттестационной комиссии)

Слушали:

§ 1. Об утверждении КЕЙЛИС-БОРОК Владимира Исааковича в ученой степени доктора физико-математических наук на основании защиты 25 ноября 1953 г. в Совете Геофизического института АН СССР диссертации: "Интерференционные сейсмические волны в слоистой среде".

Постановили:

Утвердить КЕЙЛИС-БОРОК Владимира Исааковича в ученой степени доктора физико-математических наук.

Председатель Высшей аттестационной комиссии — В.Елютин

...ретарь — И.Горшков

...ченого секретаря
...й аттестационной
комиссии

А.Сергеев

16. ноября 195 4 г.

900—1500

Doctor of Science Diploma, November 16, 1954

59

talent and allowed him a free run of his group, with only minimal influence from the Institute's officials, who, in those Communist times, had a lot of say in hiring decisions and other internal affairs. Being in this privileged position, Volodya assembled an outstanding team of young scientists. Many of them were Jewish, which made it more difficult for them to obtain good education and top jobs in science, but Volodya recognized talent and developed devious ways to cut through the red tape, hiring top young scientists for his department regardless of any other considerations about their nationality and political background. Many years later, when asked what he believed to be his top lifetime achievement, he said "I gave jobs to hundreds of Jews". He felt strongly about his team, and in return inspired devotion other leaders could only dream of.

Professor's attestation, April 21, 1965

Volodya's ability to organize teams of incredible scientists extended far beyond his department. His ideas attracted such icons of Russian mathematics as I. M. Gelfand, L. V. Kantorovich, I. I. Piatetski-Shapiro, and many others. Later, when he traveled abroad, this wave extended worldwide, with scientists in USA, France, Italy, Israel, Japan, and many other countries actively collaborating with him for many years, using this work to develop future research programs of their own. The algorithms developed by Volodya's team are widely used today for seismological surveys and data analysis in seismic centers worldwide. His work has been extended far beyond the field of geophysics and is now applied to predictions of USA presidential elections, economic recessions, socio-economic crises, and other critical events in complex systems in nature and society.

Volodya's team founded computational seismology as a new fundamental direction in geophysics. One of many applications of these basic studies was detection of underground explosions and distinguishing them from regular seismic activity by analysis of surface waves. This possibility, discovered simultaneously by Volodya and Frank Press, provided the turning point at the international technical discussions on nuclear test ban treaty (Geneva, 1959-1961), for the first time showing the world that nuclear test ban is a real possibility. Volodya was among Soviet experts at these negotiations. There, he met with distinguished American scientists. Frank Press was one of them and his meetings with Volodya initiated their fruitful scientific collaboration and friendship.

In 1964, at the height of the Cold War, Volodya, in close collaboration with Ch. Pekeris, F. Press, and L. Knopoff, organized a Working Group on Geophysical Theory and Computers, which later became the Committee on Mathematical Geophysics. This meeting, sponsored by the International Union of Geophysics and Geodesy (IUGG), attracted top scientists working in the fields of geophysics and applied mathematics. Volodya remained the chairman of this committee for 15 years, expanding its work to collaborations worldwide. In 1966 he established "Computational Seismology", a scientific journal that publishes cutting edge results in this field and is still ongoing today.

Stories from the Good Old Days

Irina Rotwain, colleague, MITPAN:

When I first saw KB (Keilis-Borok), he was sitting on the steps of the Moscow University wearing a cowboy shirt and some ridiculous pants, surrounded by men sitting next to him in suits and ties and having an intense discussion with him. This was the geophysics congress in 1970s.

I was walking with Shelya Guberman. He pointed at this youngster in a cowboy shirt and asked: "Do you want to work with him?"

"Of course!"

***

We were riding a trolley bus on our way back from the famous seminar organized and headed by I. Gelfand, the icon of Russian mathematics. The trolley bus was packed, we were barely able to get on and push through to the ticket machine. An oversized woman carrying two large grocery bags entered the trolley bus in our wake. She looked at us angrily and mumbled: "I know your sort, you can weasel your way everywhere." She raised her hand to hold on to the upper railing, so that her bag ended up on KB's head. I immediately opened my mouth to tell the woman everything I thought about her, but at that moment KB turned to her and said: "Please forgive me. I should have helped you earlier. Can I hold your bags for you?" You should have seen her face, should have heard her apologies and thanks. It was such an important lesson for me.

***

A regular working day. I am sitting in KB's office preparing materials for our latest paper. KB, at the same time, is dictating letters to his secretary (can't remember her name, let's say, Marina). One of our colleagues bursts into the office and says: "Vladimir Isaakovich! I just realized how I can prove it!..." They spend twenty minutes discussing the idea. Less than five minutes after the end of the conversation another man bursts into the office: "Vladimir Isaakovich! You are absolutely wrong! This has to be done in a completely different way!" Followed by another twenty minutes, discussing why KB is wrong.

Marina is getting upset. When a third colleague runs in, Marina cannot take it anymore: "How can you do this?" she asks the man. "Can't you see Vladimir Isaakovich is working—and you are all bursting in without knocking? How can you interfere with his important work?" The newcomer turns red with embarrassment, apologizes, and leaves.

And then KB says: "Marina, I am sitting here exactly because I want them to be able to burst in and tell me what they think. Don't you understand, they are all smarter than I am, and if they can't do this I have no place here."

MITPAN

Anna Kashina, Alexander A. Soloviev:

By 1980 Volodya's department had grown so much that it was necessary to considerably increase its working premises. A decision to supply the IPE with an additional building was made. A practical realization of this plan, however, was a rather difficult task—and Volodya and his team had taken it upon themselves.

It was out of the question to get a building in the city center, close

Volodya (third from left) and his research team during the renovation of the additional IPE building.

to the IPE. But, as it happened, through an intricate net of diplomacy enabled by Volodya's talent in dealing with officials, a building was found in the near-suburbs, sufficiently large to accommodate the department. The building required a fundamental reconstruction, but that did not stop Volodya. He enlisted support of the Academy of Sciences and mobilized his entire department, as well as a number of others recruited via his eloquence—or bribery, where needed. The team worked weekends and holidays to prepare the new building. When, in 1986, they moved in, it felt like home.

Watching a skit. In the back, left to right: A. Gabrielov, A. Zelevisky, O. Gotsadze. In the front: Lucia (right) and S. Malinovskaya (left). This picture was taken during the IPE days.

After moving to the new building, the department continued to be in progress and an idea had arisen to turn it into a new institute of the Academy of Sciences. Again, Volodya's amazing ability to cut through the red tape served him well. He managed to achieve a nearly unprecedented victory, available only to select few: he got strong support from G. I. Marchuk, the President of the Academy of Sciences at the time, and in July 1989 a Government decision was made to open the Institute. It is said that this decision coincided with the successful prediction of the Lima Prieta earthquake in California by Volodya's team, which was reported to Gorbachev and served as a highlight in his communications with Ronald Reagan. The Institute became Volodya's reward for this triumph of the Soviet science and politics.

Volodya named his new institute "International Institute of Earthquake Prediction Theory and Mathematical Geophysics" (which became widely known by its Russian abbreviation—MITPAN).

The institute became Volodya's second home—or perhaps the first one, since his work always came first. He took great pride in it, and felt bonded with his colleagues, old and new, whom he treated

During a skit: Irina Rotwain presenting Volodya with papers. Left to right: V. Pisarenko, I. Rotwain, T. Zhelankina, G. Kovaleva, G. Molchan, E. Vilkovich, T. Kronrod, V. Aver'yanova. This picture was taken in the temporary building on Prospect Mira, which Volodya's department occupied before their move to Varshavskoe Shosse.

like extended family. They continued and expanded on their traditions developed during their IPE days of non-stop work on exciting scientific problems. They also continued holding amazing holiday parties, where they often staged plays and concerts, laughing together about the good times. These concerts were where the song was created and often used: "We have solved so many problems and scientific tasks, but nothing can satisfy this impossible man, Keilis-Borok!"

In 1998 Volodya was 76 and had to lay down his directorship because of the age limitation imposed by the Russian Academy of Sciences. His successor A. A. Soloviev, who worked in Volodya's Department, then Institute, since the end of 1976, maintains the focus of the Institute on preserving and expanding not only the major scientific directions initiated by Volodya in the early 1960's, but also the spirit of bonding and camaraderie that continues to make the Institute a unit, powerful and vibrant with its fundamental scientific traditions. During the first several years Volodya ensured strong and invaluable support for the new director. When Volodya finally moved abroad permanently he maintained close ties with his Institute.

Surface Wave Seismology

Anatoly Levshin, colleague, University of Colorado:

I graduated from the Department of Geology of the Moscow State University in 1954 and for seven years worked in the field of seismic prospecting of shallow depths with civil engineering applications. My studies of seismic surface waves started around 1960, when, during the field seismic experiments, I discovered that many important properties of the upper layers of the Earth crust may be determined from surface wave records. My poor knowledge of the surface wave theory led me to contact people working in this field. After a chance meeting with Vladimir Keilis-Borok (VKB) at a skating rink in Mos-

A. Levshin (left) with his wife (middle) and Volodya (right) in 2001

cow and a short talk with him, I was invited to participate in his seminar at the Institute of Physics of the Earth (IPE). Several visits to this seminar and follow-up meetings at his home resulted in an invitation to join his group at IPE. I was very flattered, and soon after getting my PhD from IPE on my work in civil engineering, I became a member of his group in 1962. Since that time we worked together until my emigration to the USA at the end of 1991, where I continued my work on surface wave seismology at the University of Colorado, Boulder.

VKB's small group at IPE soon became a laboratory, later a department, and eventually (in 1986) the Institute of Theory of Earthquake Prediction and Mathematical Geophysics (MITPAN). All this progress had been made due to VKB's incredible energy and his strong drive to create a new branch of geophysics—computational geophysics. Working together with VKB and soon becoming his deputy, I was able to fully appreciate his talent as a scientist, an inexhaustible generator of new ideas and an indomitable fighter for new approaches to the analysis of geophysical data. He could be quite arrogant and obstinate when his ideas were met with resistance of the academic bureaucracy. He was able to attract the most prominent

Tanya Levshina (A. Levshin's daughter) with Volodya in 2001

mathematicians to the development of new approaches in geophysics: I. Gelfand, L. Kantorovich, I. Pyatecki-Shapiro, and to recruit several talented young mathematicians to our department who made remarkable contributions to solving problems of computational geophysics. Due to close contacts with prominent geophysicists abroad and permanent efforts to overcome bureaucratic barriers he was able to send many of our colleagues abroad for temporary work in the most prestigious scientific centers of the USA, United Kingdom, France, Italy, Norway, etc. I should also mention that VKB's care about his colleagues and their well-being was extraordinary. It was completely unusual for the academic atmosphere of that time.

From here on I want to discuss his contributions to surface wave theory and its interpretations, as I learned so much from him in the time of our joint work in this field.

It is difficult to provide an accurate historical overview in this short article and to fully reflect the studies that enriched the theory and practice in this area. However, it is important to note the key contributions by VKB, the author of the first fundamental study on the excitation and propagation of interferential seismic waves in multilayered media [1]. He developed the concept about the differences in the spectra of seismic waves created by shallow earthquakes and underground explosions, which served as the foundation of the modern methodology of detection of underground explosions (the so-called mb:Ms discriminant) [2-4]. He initiated the use of spectral theory of differential operators in the analysis of the interference wave fields in vertically inhomogeneous media. This led to the development of effective methods for calculation and analysis of the surface waves in realistic models of the Earth [5,6]. V. Keilis-Borok was the first to formulate the general idea of inverse problems in seismology [7] and initiated the effective methodology of construction of the velocity profiles of the Earth from the combined seismological data (travel times and amplitudes of the body waves and dispersion curves of the surface waves). He led national and international projects on the applications of this methodology to the studies of the Earth structure in different regions of the world [8-10]. It is difficult to overstate the significance of these studies to the development of surface wave seismology.

Of course, the modern surface wave seismology is far ahead compared to the early time when VKB was deeply involved in its development and applications. Further developments in the theory of surface waves in 3D-models of the Earth, the revolution in digital seismometry, major expansion of global and regional seismic networks, achievements in data availability and computers power, new technologies of seismic tomography, discoveries of opportunities to use ambient seismic noise—all of this drastically changed the ability to use surface waves in studies of the Earth and brought many fundamental results in understanding of the Earth's structure and tectonic history [12-18]. I refer here only to a few selected works, in which I have participated, as the list of publication on modern surface wave seismology is tremendous. But the role of V.I. Keilis-Borok as one of initiators of these revolutionary changes will be always remembered.

1. Keilis-Borok, V.I., 1960. Interferential surface waves. Akad. Nauk SSSR, 160p. (in Russian).

2. Keilis-Borok, V.I., 1959. On estimation of the displacement in an earthquake source and of source dimensions. Annali di Geofisica, Vol. XII, n. 2, pp.205-214.

3. Keilis-Borok, V.I. 1959-1961, 1987. Series of papers on nuclear explosion recognition. Proc. Geneva conference of technical experts for verification of compliance to Nuclear Test Ban Treaty.

4. Keilis-Borok, V.I., 1960. Difference of surface waves spectrum for earthquakes and underground explosions. Proc. of the Inst. Physics of the Earth Ac. Sci. USSR, No 15, 8p. (in Russian).

5. Keilis-Borok, V.I., Neigauz, M.G., Shkadinskaya, G.V., 1965. Application of the theory of eigenfunctions to the calculations of surface wave velocities. Review of Geophysics, Vol. 3, No 1, pp.105-109.

6. Andrianova, Z.A., Keilis-Borok, V.I., Levshin, A.L., Neigauz, M.G., 1967. Seismic Surface Love Waves. Consultants Bureau, New York.

7. Keilis-Borok, V.I., 1964. Seismology and logics. In: Research in Geophysics. Vol. 2, The M.I.T. Press, pp.61-79.

8. Keilis-Borok, V.I. and Yanovskaya, T.B., 1967. Inverse problems of seismology (structural review). Geophys. J.R. Astr. Soc. 13, pp.223-234.

9. Valus, V.P., Keilis-Borok, V.I., Levshin, A.L., 1969. Determination of the velocity profile of the upper mantle in Europe. Doklady Academii Nauk SSSR, 185, No. 3, 564-567.

10. Keilis-Borok, V.I., 1971. The inverse problem of seismology. In: Mantle and Core in Planetary Physics, Academic Press Inc., New York, pp.242-274.

11. Keilis-Borok, V.I., Editor, 1987. The surface seismic waves in laterally-inhomogeneous media (in Russian: Nauka, Moscow); (in English: Kluwer Acad. Publishers, Dordrecht.1989).

12. Ritzwoller, M.H., and A.L. Levshin, 1998, Surface wave tomography of Eurasia: group velocities, J. Geophys. Research, 103, 4839-4878.

13. Barmin, M.P., M.H. Ritzwoller, and A.L. Levshin, 2001. A fast and reliable method for surface wave tomography, PAGEOPH, 158, n.8, 1351-1375.

14. Levshin, A.L., and M.H. Ritzwoller, 2001, Surface waves in seismology and sesimic prospecting, Computational Seismology, 32, 27-32 (Moscow, GEOS, in Russian).

15. Ritzwoller, M.H., N.M. Shapiro, M.P. Barmin, and A.L. Levshin, 2002, Global surface wave diffraction tomography, J. Geoph. Res., 107 , B12,2335,doi:10.1029, 2002JB001777.

16. Bensen, G.D, M.H. Ritzwoller, M.P. Barmin, A.L. Levshin, F. Lin, M.P. Moschetti, N.M. Shapiro, and Y. Yang, 2006. Process-

ing seismic ambient noise data to obtain reliable broad-band sur-face wave dispersion measurements, Geophys. J. Int., 169, 1239-1260, doi: 10.1111/j.1365-246X.2007.03374.x.

17. Levshin, A.L., J. Schweitzer, C. Weidle, N. Shapiro, and M. Ritz-woller, 2007. Surface Wave Tomography of the Barents Sea and Surrounding Regions, Geophys. J. Int., 170, p. 441-459, doi:10.1111/j.1365-246X.2006.03285.x.

18. Panza, J.F., C. Doglioni, and A.L. Levshin, 2010. Assymetric oce-anic basins, Geology, 38, n. 1, 59-62, doi: 10.1130/G30570.1.

Surface Wave Tomography

From the article by Tatyana B. Yanovskaya "The development of methods of surface wave tomography."

In 1950s seismologists began to display interest in using surface waves for solving different seismology problems—determination of the structure of the Earth crust and upper mantle, localization of lateral heterogeneities on different scales, study of earthquake sources, and discrimination between records from explosions and earthquakes. The well-developed theory of surface waves and the methods for computing fields of these waves were needed for tackling these problems. V. I. Keilis-Borok understood this and devoted himself to development such theory for layered media. His Doctor of Science thesis resulted from these studies and he intended to publish it as a book titled "Interferential Surface Waves" [1]. He involved me in editing this book and so I became acquainted with Vladimir Isaakovich. The work was rather bulky, because the manuscript contained a lot of formulas that needed to be examined carefully. During this work I have acquired a steady interest to the theory of surface waves.

T. B. Yanovskaya

In 1960s-1970s, V. I. Keilis-Borok became interested in inverse problems in seismology [2, 3]. In those years, rapid growth of this area of geophysics was due, on one hand, to the accumulation of large quantities of data and on the other—to the emergence of computers. At the same time a key question that bothered everyone was whether the inverse problems in geophysics have unique solutions. This was due to the limitations of the data used, observation mistakes, and the nature of the data.

As soon as the first publications by Backus and Gilbert appeared on this topic at the end of 1960s, V. I. Keilis-Borok turned his attention to this problem. He immediately realized that the method proposed in these publications is highly promising in applications to different areas of geophysics, especially seismology. Under his guidance, my group began to develop new methods for solution of inverse problems aimed at horizontal irregularities of the Earth. Indeed, these ideas proved to be very fruitful for solving the inverse problems in seismology, tomography in particular, based on the data about dispersion of the surface waves. In the last four decades this method, termed Backus-Gilbert method, became widely spread in both regional and global studies of lateral irregularities of the structure of the Earth crust and upper mantle.

As a result, my scientific interests are focused on the problems that have been raised by Vladimir Isaakovich—the theory of surface waves and surface wave tomography. He was always vividly interested in my achievements, helped me in difficult situations, and his advice was always utterly valuable to me.

1. V. I. Keilis-Borok. 1960. Interferential Surface Waves. Ac. Sci. USSR. Moscow. 194 p. (in Russian)

2. V. I. Keilis-Borok, T. B. Yanovskaya. 1967. Inverse problems of seismology (structural review). Geoph.J.R. astr.Soc, 13, 223-234

3. V. I. Keilis-Borok. 1971. Inverse problems of seismology. In: Mantle and Core in Planetary Physics. L Corso, Acad.Press Inc, New York, 242-274.

Computational Seismology

Vladlen Pisarenko, colleague, MITPAN:

> Each discipline is only scientific to the degree to which it can be defined by mathematics.
>
> D. Maxwell

Vladimir Isaakovich Keilis-Borok is the creator of a new scientific field—the modern mathematical geophysics—and the founder of a school of scientists who are developing it.

V. Pisarenko

The main focus of mathematical geophysics is application of modern advances in mathematics to the problems of geophysics. In particular, Vladimir Isaakovich and his team worked on the following tasks:

- standardization and analysis of large seismological datasets

- development of artificial intelligence in seismological applications

- development of the methods of seismic risk assessment

- application of pattern recognition theory and the modern methods of nonlinear dynamics to earthquake prediction

One of the most important works by Vladimir Isaakovich, his scientific credo, is the paper titled "Seismology and Logics", published in 1964. In this paper, Vladimir Isaakovich for the first time approached the biggest challenge of seismology in early 1960's: processing and interpretation of the increasing flood of information, incoming from the global network of seismological stations newly created at the time. Vladimir Isaakovich saw the only possible solution to this challenge in "standardization and formalization of the increasing number of elements in the work of seismologists and incorporation of probabilistic connections into wider areas". This solution seems obvious to us today, but at the time it looked like a revolution in seismology.

To solve the problems in the newly created field of computational geophysics, Vladimir Isaakovich mobilized a large group of famous Russian mathematicians. Many of the joint papers written by this team founded their own areas of computational geophysics. Among these mathematicians were L. V. Kantorovich, I. M. Gelfand, G. I. Petrashen', A. Y. Povzner, I. I. Pyatetskii-Shapiro, Y. G. Sinai, A. M. Yaglom, A. S. Monin, E. M. Landis, M. G. Neigauz, and many others.

Vladimir Isaakovich not only collaborated with prominent scientists, but also staffed his own department at the Institute of Earth Physics with young talented mathematicians. For a long time the main source of these talents was the Department of Mechanics and Mathematics at the Moscow State University, the best institution in the Soviet Union. This strategy may have seemed risky, since the main directions of Vladimir Isaakovich's institute were geophysics and seismology. But Vladimir Isaakovich firmly believed in mathematics and mathematicians, and the results obtained by his team demonstrate that this belief was well justified. Among the graduates of the Department of Mathematics and Mechanics at MSU, one can name such scientists as B. M. Naimark, V. F. Pisarenko, V. M. Markushevich, M. L. Gerver, G. M. Molchan, E. L. Reznikov, and many others.

Vladimir Isaakovich's papers were always characterized by clear, condensed, expressive language and exceptional clarity, which reflected his clarity of thoughts and scientific concepts. These papers serve as a great example to young scientists. It is possible that his distinctive style was influenced by the poetry of Boris Pasternak, his favorite poet he always loved to quote to his colleagues.

Seismic Risk Assessment

George Molchan, colleague, MITPAN:

Before 1960s, seismic risk was characterized by the maximum magnitude of possible tremors at a given point, I_{max} (g). The frequency of repetition of this maximum tremor at different points of a uniform I-zone could vary by orders of magnitude, however this knowledge did not affect the global construction planning. The scale of earthquake damage could be so great, and the insurance so imperfect that no country in the world was truly ready for economic evaluation of seismic risk.

In 1960s USSR started implementing global construction projects, which facilitated the need of evaluation of seismic risk from the economic standpoint. V. I. Keilis-Borok and S. V. Medvedev were the first to realize this. In 1962 they suggested a new parameter of seismic risk: the repetition of tremors, or, in modern terminology, "co-tremors". V. I. Keilis-Borok developed a method to calculate both the tremors and their average economic effect. Thus, a new discipline of seismic risk was created, uniting seismology, tectonics, and major tremor detection with economics and demographics.

The purely seismological side of seismic risk became the long-term research focus of Y.V. Riznichenko, the corresponding member of the Academy of Sciences of the USSR, and his school. As for the applications, many realized that in the framework of Puasson's hypothesis about the earthquake flow, tremors enable probabilistic estimation of the distribution of earthquake intensity in a given point over a fixed period of time. This enabled the transition from calculating average losses from earthquake to calculating the distribution of losses at a given point, which is much more useful from the engineering point of view.

Despite the promise of the new method, it also had flaws, revealed during the construction of the Baikal-Amur Transsiberian Railway (BAM, in Russian: Baikalo-Amurskaya Magistral'). In 1968, the project was being evaluated. The railway, planned to be 980 km long, was supposed to go through a high seismicity zone, requiring an economic evaluation of creation of anti-seismic reinforcements for the tracks. Presented as "the project of the century", the railway required a more precise evaluation of seismic risk than could not be provided by either the average or the point-by-point estimation of damage. It was necessary to also estimate the dependence of the low-probability total losses on the type of anti-seismic reinforcements

G. Molchan (Zhora, left) and Volodya (right) visiting Castel Gandolfo during the meeting of the Pontifical Academy of Sciences, 2004

over time. This was a unique task in engineering.

M. A. Sadovsky realized the importance of this challenge and posed it to Keilis-Borok, who, with his special talent to create teams uniquely suited for each task assembled a highly balanced group to solve it in 1969. It was a group of mathematicians and computer programmers with the added expertise from L. V. Kantorovich in economics and I. L. Nersesov in seismicity, plus the project engineers who consulted the teams on anti-seismic measures. The conclusion of the team seemed paradoxical at the time: despite the paleo-data evidence of catastrophic earthquakes in the region, it did not prove economically feasible to employ anti-seismic reinforcements.

V. I. Keilis-Borok's initiative transformed the new approaches developed during the BAM task into a general probabilistic concept of seismic risk, applicable to the analysis of many economical and social problems related to seismicity. The methodology they developed considerably broadened and unified the existing methods of risk assessment. It was successfully tested in application to regions of Italy and Caucasis and used to advance the goals of UNESCO of analyzing the seismic risk in highly populated cities all over the world, as well as to optimizing the insurance stakes in seismically active regions.

Today, we can definitely say that Keilis-Borok's works turned around the guarded, often negative, attitude toward seismic risk assessment, into a well-realized economic necessity worldwide.

Working Abroad

Anna Kashina:

Volodya's gift of connecting with people, taking deep interest in everyone he met and inspiring openness, did not always expand into his own personal life. He had many friends and followers, but very few with whom he could ever feel true spiritual closeness. He often felt lonely and depressed, and his life in Moscow, with constant worries, with the need to overcome constant restrictions and everyday problems, did not leave much time for him to enjoy himself.

A new window opened to him when he was first allowed to go abroad. The freedom he felt during those brief times instantly overwhelmed him. These trips became a window into the world he always wanted to belong to: the marvels of the Italian art, the eerie beauty

Volodya on a trip abroad

of Venice, the living history of London, the free spirit of Paris, the skyscrapers of New York. These were the worlds he read about in his favorite books, the places of true freedom where he could say and do anything he wanted.

Unlike at home, this sense of liberation drove him to form many instantly deep friendships that became his comfort and the focus of his emotions for many years to come.

All this became possible for him when his work on seismic waves earned him a place among the very select team of scientific experts from the USSR at the Geneva talks on the nuclear test ban treaty in 50-60ths. His findings on seismic wave detection, as it turned out, had a very practical application: to detect underground nuclear explosions and distinguish them from regular seismic activity, enabling monitoring of nuclear explosions worldwide.

The fact that someone could actually tell the difference was a novelty, and a very timely one. At that time, the world superpowers were trying to come to an agreement on limitations of the nuclear tests, and Volodya's work, along with that of his colleagues, provided true means of enforcing a nuclear test ban treaty between the world's superpowers. Thus, Volodya not only ended up going abroad—a seeming impossibility for a man of his background in the Soviet times—but also a focus of attention from the world's best scientists.

Billie and Frank Press

On his very first trip to Geneva Volodya met several people who became his lifelong friends, some of the closest he ever had. Among them was an American seismologist Frank Press, whose work on seismic waves was complementary to Volodya's. This was the beginning of an amazing friendship that lasted until the end of Volodya's life. Frank and his wife Billie became like a second family to Volodya, people who represented everything he wanted to be, who connected with him so deeply on the intellectual and the emotional level.

Frank and Billie Press introduced Volodya to their friends, who became part of Volodya's expanding circle and participated in many of his international collaborations and close personal interactions. I have never known anyone closer to Volodya than both of the Presses, each in their own way. Volodya admired Frank's sharp mind,

Volodya and Frank Press

his subtle humor, his broad knowledge, his sophisticated, laconic style that Volodya always tried to mirror. He connected with Billie more on the emotional level, in awe of her life force, her openness, her deep insight into his feelings and thoughts. In a way, he was in love with each of them, and this love lasted for the rest of his life. He felt their joys and sorrows nearly as keenly as they did. He felt nearly the same pride as Billie and Frank did when watching the academic success of their son Bill. He became a friend and confidant of their daughter Paula. Both my mother and I always felt that these people were part of our family too—distant geographically, but as caring and involved in out lives as our own relatives.

Regular trips abroad, interactions with Billie, Frank, and the people who knew them, became an important part of Volodya's world, feeding both his science and his emotional comfort. These trips sharply contrasted with the way things went for him in Moscow, where his closest friend Volodya Barlas, and others, including A. Monin, G. Barenblat, the artist Yu. Vasiliev, drifted away from him. In 1982, Volodya Barlas died, hit by a bicycle and knocking his head on the corner of a stone curb. Despite the fact that their friendship

Volodya and Billie Press in Washington, D.C.

was not always smooth and often emotionally draining, his death shook Volodya deeply and left a vacuum he could not possibly fill. His daughter Ira had her own family, and I was too young. His wife, Lucia, never became the close companion he needed. In these circumstances, his trips abroad became the only times he could approach happiness, the only times he could let himself go.

Thus began his wishing that our whole family could move abroad, first a dream, then, after the fall of the Soviet Union—a reality. He felt so happy when first my parents, then I, moved to the United States. For a while he remained behind, then followed us in 1998—alas, too late to fully adapt to the American life.

He was 77 when he received his first stable position at UCLA.

***

From recollections by Frank and Paula Press:

Volodya and Frank met during the International Geophysical Year (IGY, 1956-1957). During that time, USA initiated a discussion on nuclear test ban treaty. The politicians could not agree on the details, and one of the biggest questions on everyone's mind was: how could we enforce such a treaty? After all, an underground nuclear test couldn't possibly be distinguished from regular seismic activity, could it?

This was where the scientists came in. Remarkably, Volodya's work on seismic waves proved that nuclear tests evoke a different wave pattern and could be distinguished from the natural Earth tremors. When the officials recognized the importance of this discovery, Volodya became famous. In the Soviet Russia, a Jewish scientist without a formal affiliation with the Communist Party had almost no chance to go abroad. But the red tape was cut for Volodya and a few of his fellow experts, who were sent to represent the Soviet scientists in technical discussions on the nuclear test ban treaty in Geneva, 1959-1961. Volodya Keilis-Borok was among the very few Soviet experts invited to these negotiations. On this trip he met his colleagues representing the American scientists, including Frank Press. This meeting was the beginning of a life-long friendship.

Paula remembers Volodya's visit to Pasadena, probably in early 1960s when Frank was still a professor at Caltech (1955-1965). She was a child, and she remembers being immediately entranced. "He had a magical ability to relate to children," she recalls, "in a way that made them feel special—like they were the center of his universe. It was that way for me, but the same for my daughter Laura and my niece Sara."

Paula remembers that Volodya was allowed to make that trip abroad because he promised to bring a heart valve for his boss's wife. I am not certain if this was the case then, or later, but this was what it often took to be allowed out of the Soviet Russia—the price that Volodya paid willingly to be able to travel and, on occasions, to bring along his close colleagues and later—my mother and father.

Paula said Volodya was like her "fairy godfather". When she was a teenager and had a difficult time with her parents, Volodya took it upon himself to visit her regularly, talk to her, meet the people she interacted with, and most importantly—listen, something she felt she wasn't getting enough of from anyone else. "Volodya's significance to me and my family cannot be overstated," she said. "Volodya was a devoted, loving friend throughout my life and came to my rescue on more than one occasion. No matter what age or stage I was at, he listened with concern and tried to do whatever he could to help. Not many friends will do that. Memories of Volodya are interwoven in the fabric of my life and in that regard he remains vital, enriching and cherished.

"He was also deeply loved by my mother and was, perhaps, her closest friend. Volodya was the source of great happiness and joy for her—often at times when she was otherwise unhappy and depressed. Their mutual affection and admiration was deep and enduring. I think in many ways they were soul mates.

"When he was younger, my dad was never one to develop close friendships, but Volodya was an exception. As a colleague and a friend, Volodya mattered deeply to my dad."

Volodya and Billie

Frank remembered how Billie and Volodya traveled together in Europe, just the two of them, retracing the steps of the Napoleon army. Paula could not recall this trip, but she commented how she was always amazed at the way Volodya and Billie connected with each other, fulfilling the need for the emotional closeness that no one else could possibly match.

When Billie turned 70, Volodya and I visited her in Washington, D.C. His gift to her, which he asked me to prepare, was a printed, framed poem by Lord Byron, "Stanzas to Augusta". He felt very personal about this gift, which, on some level, summarized many of the things she was for him:

George Gordon, Lord Byron, "Stanzas to Augusta"

1

Though the day of my destiny's over,
And the star of my fate hath declined,
Thy soft heart refused to discover
The faults which so many could find;
Though thy soul with my grief was acquainted,
It shrunk not to share it with me,
And the love which my spirit hath painted
It never hath found but in thee.

2

Then when nature around me is smiling
The last smile which answers to mine,
I do not believe it beguiling
Because it reminds me of thine;
And when winds are at war with the ocean,
As the breasts I believed in with me,
If their billows excite an emotion
It is that they bear me from thee.

3

Though the rock of my last hope is shiver'd,
And its fragments are sunk in the wave,
Though I feel that my soul is deliver'd
To pain—it shall not be its slave.
There is many a pang to pursue me:

They may crush, but they shall not contemn—
They may torture, but shall not subdue me—
'Tis of thee that I think—not of them.

4

Though human, thou didst not deceive me,
Though woman, thou didst not forsake,
Though loved, thou forborest to grieve me,
Though slander'd, thou never could'st shake,—
Though trusted, thou didst not betray me,
Though parted, it was not to fly,
Though watchful, 'twas not to defame me,
Nor, mute, that the world might belie.

5

Yet I blame not the world, nor despise it,
Nor the war of the many with one—
If my soul was not fitted to prize it
'Twas folly not sooner to shun:
And if dearly that error hath cost me,
And more than I once could foresee,
I have found that, whatever it lost me,
It could not deprive me of thee.

6

From the wreck of the past, which hath perish'd,
Thus much I at least may recall,
It hath taught me that what I most cherish'd
Deserved to be dearest of all:
In the desert a fountain is springing,
In the wide waste there still is a tree,
And a bird in the solitude singing,
Which speaks to my spirit of thee.

Mapping the Sites of Strong Earthquakes

Elizaveta Ranzman, colleague:

From the article "The sites of strong earthquakes: formulating the task and the method of its solution."

> "The known is known only to a few"
> —Aristotle

During a roundtable discussion in 1970s, Vladimir Isaakovich Keilis-Borok assembled a team of scientists from different disciplines—geophysicists, applied mathematicians, and one geographer-geomorphologist. The task he put in front of them: predicting the sites of strong earthquakes (I will refer to it as the Task).

V.I. Keilis-Borok directed the team to create a map of tectonically active faults in Pamir and Tian-Shan mountains. The map defined longitudinal and transversal linear zones, which were ranked according to the uniformity of the areas bordered by these zones. Territories with uniform relief were termed "blocks" and the boundaries of these blocks were assigned third rank. The boundaries of megablocks received second rank. Mountain areas with common history of the relief formation uniting several megablocks were bordered by tectonic zones of the first rank. Areas of the crossing of the zones—nodes—were circled.

Later, following a suggestion by I. P. Gerasimov, the founder of the morphostructure doctrine, the boundaries of the blocks were renamed into "morphostructural lineaments", crosses of the boundaries—into "morphostructural nodes", and the whole system—into "morphostructural zoning" (MZ).

V.I. Keilis-Borok recruited the famous Russian mathematician I. M. Gelfand and his colleague Sh. A. Guberman, with the idea of applying pattern recognition theory to the Task.

The objects for pattern recognition had been defined—morphostructural nodes, the likely areas of highest geological instability. Their characteristics were measured within circles with the radius of 40 km and centers in the intersections of lineament axial lines. The pattern recognition algorithm has been chosen—CORA-3. The characteristics of the nodes were chosen. Using computers—a novelty at the time—the characteristics of the two groups of nodes had been obtained: "dangerous" (highly seismic) nodes, and "non-dangerous" (lowly seismic) nodes. The results of this study were published in 1972 in the journal *"Reports of the Academy of Sciences of the USSR"* [1].

Here is how the rest of the work unraveled. V. I. Keilis-Borok selected new geographical regions (after Tian-Shan and Pamir came the united region of Balkans, Asia Minor, and Trancaucasia, then California); geomorphologists (my colleagues and I) created MZ maps of these regions, each took 4-6 months. Sh. A. Guberman and his colleagues implemented pattern recognition, permanently improving this procedure.

For the work on the Task, V. I. Keilis-Borok recruited top geologists and geophysicists from the countries for which the analysis was being developed: USA, Italy, France, India. For the new territories, his younger colleagues/followers joined the study: V. Kossobokov, A. Gabrielov, I. Rotwain, A. Gvishiani, A. Soloviev, later—the geographer A. Gorshkov, and others.

I believe that the Task formulated by V.I. Keilis-Borok had been solved. The classification of the nodes into highly and lowly seismic, performed by the recognition algorithm CORA-3 based on the MZ maps, proved to be effective.

The Task utilized non-traditional methods of seismotectonics—developing a hypothesis that strong earthquake epicenters are correlated to morphostructural nodes—the intersection sites between tectonically active linear zones.

The positions of the nodes were defined using cartographic modeling of the modern block structure of the Earth crust, carried out by means of specially developed methodology—morphostructural zoning on the basis of formalized criteria that stemmed from targeted analysis of the Earth relief.

All the elements of the block structure form a unified system and cannot be considered in an isolated way: morphostructural lineaments define the boundaries of the blocks, positions of the nodes are determined by the intersections of the morphostructural lineaments.

The solution of the Task is applicable to different geographic areas at different scales. The method for the solution of the Task remains the same when the seismic threshold is reduced down to magnitude M = 5.0 or elevated to M ≥ 7.5. The criteria of highly seismic nodes recognized for one seismically active regions proved to be acceptable for defining highly seismic nodes in other regions.

The successful solution of the Task can be explained by the fact that every participant of the team, assembled and led by V. I. Keilis-Borok, was the top expert in his/her field or had enormous experience in their area of knowledge. These major stars were united by the magnitude of the Task, mutual respect, and their trust in V.I. Keilis-Borok.

The methodology developed during the solution of the Task had also been applied to several other problems. Information about 17 giant deposits of oil and natural gas was compared with the MZ map of the Andes, developed earlier for recognition of the sites of strong earthquakes (scale 1:9,000,000). 16 of these deposits turned out to be located in the morphostructural nodes—within 75 km of the intersections of lineament axial lines. Pattern recognition was used to classify these nodes, and those that seemed promising in terms of potential search for giant deposits of oil and gas were identified. In two of those, large deposits of oil and gas had been later discovered.

A two-year collaboration with geologists and geophysicists of India resulted in recognition of sites prone to strong earthquakes in the Himalayas. For the first time in practice of such studies a multi-colored MZ map of India and the neighboring territories had been published.

Systemic connection between the elements of the modern block structures—blocks, morphostructural lineaments, and morphostructural nodes—exists at different scales, from large mountain ranges and plateaus to small-block structure of morphostructural nodes. The next, likely smallest levels, would include small-block structure of "inner" nodes.

It was found that the elements of the modern block structure of the Earth crust define the spatial arrangement of the components of the geographical surface of the Earth: the placement of the boundaries of natural zones, landscapes, types of soil, are close or coincide with lineament zones of different ranks. Most of the large cities on the Russian plain are located in morphostructural nodes.

High activity of the natural processes in the nodes facilitates the number of critical events within them, at the oil and gas lines, railways, long-term constructions, and other technological sites. The detailed MZ map of Moscow, a large megapolis, shows that the largest number of technical accidents happened at the intersections of boundaries of small blocks located within the Moscow node.

Studies using the methods developed during the work on the Task were constantly discussed with V.I. Keilis-Borok and reported at the seminars of his Department and Institute.

In conclusion, the methods of studying natural processes developed during the work on the Task defined new directions of Earth sciences. Joint efforts of the scientists from different disciplines—geophysicists, geographers, mathematicians—in the process of solving the problem of earthquake-prone areas determination created methodology that is not only fruitfully used in other areas but also enables a new understanding of the connection between deep Earth processes and different aspects of Earth's geography. This is a highly promising filed.

1. Gelfand, I.M., Sh.A. Guberman, M.L. Izvekova, V.I. Keilis-Borok, and E.Ya. Ranzman, On criteria of high seismicity. *Trans. (Doklady) Acad. Sci. SSSR*, 1972, 202(6): 1317-1320.

Caltech

From recollections by Linda Pauling Kamb:

In 1978 Volodya came to Caltech as a Fairchild Scholar. His invitation came from Professor Barclay Kamb, a colleague and a friend of Frank Press—as well as, at the time, the chairman of the Division of Geology at Caltech. Barclay was interested in meeting the talented Russian scientist, but to his surprise, when he issued the prestigious Fairchild Scholar invitation, no response from Volodya came. After waiting for a while Barclay had given up, and assumed Volodya was not coming, possibly because of the issues with the Soviet government.

Then, one day, Barclay received a phone call. On the other end of the line, a man with a thick Russian accent said: "Hi, I am Volodya Keilis-Borok. I am in San Diego and will arrive at Caltech in three days".

Three days of panic ensued, when Caltech scrambled to find an apartment and a car and to make all the other arrangements for the visiting scientist. But when Volodya finally came, they were not disappointed. Barclay and his wife, Linda, became Volodya's close friends, among the very few that stayed by his

97

side until the end.

Linda remembered feeling instantly charmed when she first met Volodya. He spoke with an accent that took getting used to, but his speech was full of quotes and idioms that made it fascinating to listen to. Very soon, she also realized with amazement that this man,

Volodya at Linda and Barclay's family dinner with Linus Pauling in Pasadena, CA. Clockwise from front left: Linus Kamb, Volodya, Lucrecia Salvado, au pair girl, Sasha Kamb, Linda Kamb, Elfriede Yost (a family friend from Germany), Carlos Salvado, Linus Pauling, Ava Helen Pauling, Barclay J.Kamb (Barky), Antony Kamb (photo by Barclay Kamb).

"Keilis-Borok", as her husband Barclay used to refer to him, was the same "Volodya" her good friend Billie Press kept talking about during the annual meetings of the National Academy of Sciences in Washington, DC. A coincidence, which nevertheless made perfect sense.

When Barclay first introduced Linda to Volodya she said: "We should go out for lunch some time." His response amused her. "I thought you'd never ask!" Volodya said. Recalling this many years later, Linda said this seemed very typical for Volodya.

Volodya with friends at Caltech. Left to right: Barclay Kamb, Linda Kamb, Volodya, Diane Epstein, Samuel Epstein, Shirley Shapiro. Photo by Jerry Shapiro

Volodya took Linda on rides in his car, reciting Russian poetry to her on the way. He was a horrible driver, and he was also distracted by his own reciting. It took effort for Linda to keep her voice calm while warning him: "Look, that car in front is stopping!" Or, "This light has just turned red!" She was terrified, but not surprised, when later on Volodya had a car accident and had to stop driving. Linda believes he never drove again.

Volodya and Shirley Shapiro.

She remembers how her father, the two-time Nobel Laureate Linus Pauling, was going to

99

the Soviet Union in the early 1980s. Linda told him: "You should go see Keilis-Borok". Pauling relayed this request to the Soviet officials, and they were surprised but made the arrangements. Volodya and Pauling had an enjoyable meeting.

During Volodya's stay at Caltech in 1978, and again in 1979, as a Fairchild Scholar he became friends not only with Linda and Barclay, but also with their friends and colleagues Shirley and Jerry Shapiro, Naomi and Jerry Wasserburg, Diane and Sam Epstein. He also maintained a close friendship with Leon Knopoff, a UCLA professor and one of his original friends from the Geneva meeting in the 1960's. This friendship paved the road for his future work at UCLA, which later materialized into a faculty job he maintained until his retirement.

Volodya and colleagues at Caltech.

Linda had many fond memories about her time with Volodya. She describes him as "always such a gentleman, so old-world and charming". When he met her, he often brought her orchids. Once, walking with him at UCLA, Linda saw mistletoe in a sycamore tree above them and told him about a folk belief that if you caught a girl under a mistletoe you could kiss her. The next thing she knew, Volodya grasped her, pulled her under the mistletoe, and kissed her on the lips. They always laughed remembering that time.

When Volodya was at UCLA Linda and Barclay often drove over to meet with him and take him to lunch. After Barclay died in 2011, Linda continued on her own, first going to Westwood and later to Culver City. She stayed by his side until the end.

Predictions of the US Presidential Elections

Anna Kashina:

Volodya and his friends often had parties and dinners together, at someone's home, or in the Athenaeum, Caltech's famous faculty club. During these parties they tried to seat husbands and wives away from each other, so that they could socialize with others. Once, Volodya ended up next to a charming young woman and started telling her about his recent ideas regarding US politics. He thought he had found a way to apply his approaches to earthquake predictions to other types of events in complex systems—such as outcomes of elections in the American society. The young woman listened attentively and he got carried away, talking about the possibilities of identifying some key parameters—much like seismic activity—that would explain how choices of a president were made.

Even though the topic interested him, by his own admission he was just chatting, inspired by the attention of his dinner companion. But at the end of the meal, when everyone was allowed to stand up and mingle, she told him: "What you said was very interesting. You might want to talk to my husband, Professor Allan Lichtman, over there. He is also a Fairchild Scholar, like you, and everything you said is very relevant to his field."

When Volodya approached Allan—a handsome, dashing man that looked much too young for his distinguished position—he felt this couldn't possibly work. Yet, when he started describing his ideas he was met with unexpected attention and understanding. Allan immediately caught on, saying that the task was not actually as impossible as it seemed to Volodya at the start of the conversation. After all, to predict an outcome of a presidential election, one had to predict only one thing: which party, Republicans or Democrats, would win. In other terms, the prediction could be confined to an even simpler question: would the current ruling party stay in power, or would it be replaced?

Allan Lichtman

Volodya and Allan worked on this task very intensely. In Volodya's words, his role was easy: to use the mathematical algorithms they already had in application to another problem. Allan's was the difficult part: to identify the indicators in the society whose changes could serve as the basis of this prediction. It took deep knowledge, as well as a touch of a genius, to find the few right ones to base the prediction on. Volodya always marveled at the fact that Allan took on this project, and at Allan's knowledge and insight, so synergistic with his ideas.

After deconstructing every presidential election since 1860, they found that their outcomes were defined by how well the White House incumbent and his party had governed during a given term. Using 13 factors or "keys," they concluded that time-honored debates, speeches, rallies, platforms, or campaign tactics exerted very little influence on the outcome.

Volodya recalled this work with Allan as some of the best times he had in his life. He described how they cleaned up a big table and set it with stacks of papers related to each indicator. How they stayed up nights when needed and worked nonstop for long stretches of time. They did not have much time to work side by side during Volodya's brief visits to the US, but they utilized their time to the full.

This work became one of the most successful applications of his predictions. When applied backward to all the presidential elections in the American history, the algorithm never failed, correctly predicting the outcome of the popular vote and the outcome of each election but one, where the popular vote differed from the electoral one.

From 1980 Volodya and Allan initiated advance predictions of the presidential elections, which correctly predicted the outcome each time, months in advance of the actual event. The only exception was the election of G. W. Bush, who won against A. Gore by the electoral, but not by the popular vote in 2000. Allan is continuing these predictions.

**

Allan Lichtman:

I first met Volodya Keilis-Borok in 1981, when we were both Sherman Fairchild Visiting Distinguished Scholars at the California Institute of Technology (Cal Tech) in Pasadena, California. We were sitting together at dinner and he asked me what I did—a typical question among scholars. I replied that I was a quantitative historian who examined mathematically trends and patterns in the American past. He replied, "Oh, I do same thing." I responded, "No you don't. I am an historian and you are a geophysicist and earthquake forecaster. We couldn't possibly be doing the same thing." He explained, "You look mathematically at trends and patterns in human history, just as I do in the history of the Earth." I said, "That is very interesting, nice to meet you, goodbye." He said, "Wait." I said "Why?" He said "You and I are going to collaborate." I said, "No we're not. Earthquakes may be a big deal here in southern California, but I have to go back to American University in Washington, DC, where no one cares much about earthquakes." He said, "We are not going to collaborate on earthquakes, but on election prediction. I had fallen in love with politics when I came to America in the early 1960s as part of the Soviet scientific team working on the Nuclear Test Ban Treaty. I've always wanted to apply the methods of earthquake prediction to forecasting elections. But I live in the Soviet Union, where it is supreme leader or off with your head. You, however, are an expert in U. S. politics. With our combined expertise we could collaborate on predicting the world's most important elections, American presidential contests."

At that point I became intrigued and decided we should work together. Earthquakes and presidential elections in fact had much in common. In both cases, seemingly random and disparate events come together to produce results that are often unexpected and sometimes disastrous. Even the language of elections borrows from geophysics: we speak of political upheaval, landslide victories, and seismic shifts in voter sentiment.

Predicting earthquakes and forecasting presidential elections present similar problems. The forces and events that cause earthquakes take place far beneath the surface of the Earth, where they cannot be seen. Even if scientists could see them, the theories of earthquakes are so weak that it would be difficult to construct a causal model of them to determine precisely what effects millions of subterranean events would have on one another in different geological settings. Similarly, political analysts cannot know all the factors being weighed in the minds of voters, and even if they could, election theories do not allow them to ascertain how those factors influence millions of individuals and translate on the Election Day into the triumph of one candidate over another.

In earthquake prediction, instead of looking for "causes" that cannot be seen or measured anyway, Volodya studied what could be observed as changes in the physical environment, such as the opening of small fissures in the Earth and occurrences of minor tremors, to see if a pattern of circumstances could be discerned that would indicate an impending quake. This process is based on a mathematical technique known as "pattern recognition." Perhaps, Volodya suggested, the algorithms of pattern recognition also could disclose a relationship between distinctive features of the political environment and the outcomes of U.S. presidential elections. After all, election predictors would have substantial advantages over earthquake forecasters: we already know when and where the next election will take place; the American two-party system has remained highly stable for more than a hundred years; and the "rules" of presidential elections are all specified in advance.

In addition, I had developed a theory of presidential elections that Volodya's methodology could test. From my studies of nineteenth and twentieth century elections, I had come to embrace a "perform-ance" theory of voting in American presidential contests. Voters were not as fickle or indecisive as the polls would suggest, nor did they simply support candidates of their favorite party or responded pri-marily to such abstract considerations as political ideology or issue positions. The American electorate instead was pragmatic, reacting to the varied circumstances of each election. Simply put, the voters re-warded achievement and punished failure. But no analyst had devel-oped consistent criteria for measuring their collective assessment of incumbent performance. What were the relevant factors to be con-sidered? What were the thresholds for gauging success and failure? When did the party in power cross the line separating victory from defeat? Had the standards, by which the electorate chooses winners and losers, shifted in response to changing times, or had they re-mained stable?

To try to answer these questions, we applied pattern recognition methodology to the circumstances surrounding the 31 presidential elections that had taken place since 1860, the first year in which Re-publicans and Democrats had competed against one another as can-didates of the nation's two major political parties.

Historical evidence suggested that the incumbent party candidate, whether he was the sitting president or not, got the credit or blame for the record of the previous four years. For example, in 1896, dur-ing the most severe depression to that point in history, Democratic nominee William Jennings Bryan had repudiated the failed economic policies of his party's president, Grover Cleveland, but Bryan still had been held accountable for the "Democratic depression". Similarly, in 1920, the nominee of the incumbent Democrats, Ohio Governor James Cox, had campaigned during a recession that clearly had led to defections from the party's ranks. But the greatest proportional de-fection by far was among German Americans and Italian Americans, unhappy with the results of Woodrow Wilson's post-World War I peace settlements. Although Cox, as governor of Ohio, obviously had

had nothing to do with foreign affairs, his candidacy clearly had suffered from the failure of Wilson's peacemaking policies.

Consequently, we reframed elections in geophysical terms, not as Republicans versus Democrats, liberals versus conservations, or candidate versus candidate, but as stability versus upheaval. Stability meant that the party holding the White House prevailed in the election; upheaval meant that the challenging party prevailed. Just as the question in earthquake prediction is whether seismic stability or upheaval will prevail, the central question on the Election Day is whether there will be stability or upheaval in the White House. Will the electorate vote to retain or reject the incumbent party? America's relatively stable two-party system since 1860 facilitated this research.

The features of the political environment to be examined for all 31 elections were put in the form of questions that could be answered yes or no prior to an election. This binary approach, unique in election forecasting but common in earthquake prediction, would allow for the consideration of factors, such as foreign policy successes and failures, which could not readily be quantified but could be recognized as critical events when viewed in a historical context. The questions, or variables, would cover circumstances consistent with an incumbent performance theory of elections, as well as factors suggested by other theories.

The initial list of variables comprised some thirty questions dealing with domestic and foreign policy issues, candidate and party ideology, the unity and strength of the major parties, past election results, whether the nation was at war or peace, economic performance, policy change, social unrest, presidential scandal, campaign finance, candidates' personality traits, third party activities, vice presidential nominations, campaign strategy, and the number of consecutive terms the incumbent party had been in office all factors that might theoretically affect the outcome of elections. These variables were examined for each of the 31 elections to determine whether each one individually was consistently associated with either victory or defeat for the party in power. Some questions had such a weak relationships to presidential results including whether elections took place in times of war or peace, the stature of vice presidential nominees and the regional balance they brought to their tickets, and the dominant political party of an era—that we dropped them from the pattern recognition test.

From the remaining questions, a simple pattern recognition algorithm identified a combination of twelve variables, or "keys",' that, with but a single error, distinguished between the popular vote winners and losers in all 31 elections from 1860 to 1980. When six or more questions were answered "no" (that is, when six or more keys were discrepant, or did not favor the incumbent party), the incumbent party lost every time; when five or fewer questions were answered "no", the incumbent party won, except in 1912. The use of more powerful pattern recognition programs weighting the variables and combining them into multiple factor questions did not eliminate the error. We ultimately eliminated the error when, aided by a suggestion from Harry N. Davey—a statistician with the Bureau of Labor Statistics, we added a final thirteenth variable. These are the now famous Thirteen Keys to the White House.

Although our analysis was only retrospective at this point, the Keys revealed important insights into the American history. They showed that from the horse and buggy days of American politics when Abraham Lincoln won election in 1860 to the modern era of polls, jet planes, and television, when Ronald Reagan prevailed in 1980, the American electorate has followed a common pragmatic logic of presidential choice. The discovery of such a consistent historical pattern indicated that the American electorate demands a certain threshold level of performance and initiative from presidents. Our results showed that speeches, campaign events, debates, and fundraising, the usual focus of electoral analysis, mattered little or not at all in the final outcome of the elections. An incumbent administration risks retribution at the polls if it fails to maintain economic growth, domestic and international stability, and integrity in the conduct of government. Beyond these standards of satisfactory performance, the electorate responds positively to successful initiatives both at home and abroad, and to leaders of extraordinary stature or personal appeal.

Our first predictive test to the Keys to the White House came in April 1982, about two and half years before the upcoming presidential election. In an article published in the Washingtonian Magazine, we successfully predicted that President Ronald Reagan would be reelected in 1984. Retrospectively, the prediction of a Reagan victory may seem like any easy call, but that was hardly the case in early 1982. The economy was mired in the worst regression since the 1930s, Reagan's approval ratings were similar to those of Jimmy Carter, who he had defeated in 1980, and the president was more than 70-years-old. He would be the oldest president in US history seeking reelection.

Since 1984,the Keys system has since correctly forecast the popular vote winner of all subsequent seven presidential elections through 2012, once again often years prior to Election Day and often in contradiction to the polls. For example, the Keys forecast George H. W. Bush's 1988 victory in the late spring of that year, when Bush trailed Democratic candidate Michael Dukakis by 17 points in the polls. The Keys correctly predicted the outcome of the difficult-to-call 2004 election in April 2003. In early 2006, the Keys already forecast a Democratic victory in 2008, regardless of the identity of the major party nominees. The Keys forecast Obama very difficult reelection in January 2010, the earliest call yet. Media worldwide has extensively covered these predictions.

Thus, it is governing, not campaigning, that counts in deciding presidential elections. No party has an enduring hold on the American presidency. Moreover, political leaders need not move to the ideological center. As demonstrated by presidents such as Franklin Roosevelt and Ronald Reagan, a strong ideology can guide domestic and foreign policy initiatives that keep in line the keys needed to retain the White House. Given that campaigns don't decide elections, the Keys model also indicates that candidates should abandon conventional politics and develop the themes, issues and grassroots support needed for effective governance during the next four years. Volodya and I during more than 25 years of collaboration have sought to convince political leaders and analysts of this very important lesson.

The forecasting profession initially regarded the Keys system with great skepticism: it seemed too simple and combined fixed parameters, such as changes in per-capita GDP, with judgmental parameters, such as whether the administration holding the White House has achieved major policy change. In recent years, however, forecasters have come to accept and even celebrate the Keys. They have come to recognize that the use of simple, integral parameters is often the best way to understand complex systems and predict future outcomes. I have twice keynoted the International Forecasting Summit and published articles on the Keys in leading forecasting journals. Len Tashman, Editor of the Journal of Applied Forecasting said, "On the influence of the Keys model more generally, I think the main effect has been, to establish 'index models' as a serious approach to forecasting. The forecasting profession, like other technical fields, has grown increasing complex, with the correlation between complexity and performance quite suspect. 'Returning to basics' is always a helpful guidepost and I think the success of the Keys has given this path a boost."

In addition, the Keys approach demonstrates an effective way of combining statistical and judgmental inputs to create a forecast. And it does so in a way that emphasizes the requirement for precision in the interpretation of specific information as well as in how pieces of information are combined to form an overall picture.

Our relationship with Volodya quickly evolved into a personal one that lasted more than thirty years. I visited Volodya several times in Moscow and he visited me when he came to Washington, DC for meetings of the National Academy of Sciences. Occasionally he stayed at our home in Bethesda, Maryland just outside of DC. I traveled to Lima, Peru and Banf, Canada to meet with Volodya while he was on research trips to these places. We also collaborated on several papers and articles beyond the initial studies on the Keys to the White House. I came to know and love his family and he fully reciprocated.

In recent years Volodya, myself and other collaborators have been seeking universal application of the theory and method underlying the Keys to the White House. We were contemplating writing a book with the audacious title, "The Theory of Everything". Unfortunately, this project remained incomplete at the time of Volodya's death.

From Mathematics to
Geophysics and Back to Mathematics

From recollections by Andrei Gabrielov, colleague, Purdue University:

It was Moscow, 1973. Andrei was finishing up his graduate school at the Department of Mechanics and Mathematics (MekhMat) of the Moscow State University (MSU), the very top school in the Soviet Union. Andrei was one of the top students in his class, and has already published several papers that became seminal publications in his area. However, jobs for mathematicians, especially for those of Jewish origin, were hard to find. Andrei's teacher, the legendary mathematician I.M. Gelfand, offered to help him find a good position. Andrei wanted to focus on scientific research, and Gelfand introduced him to Volodya Keilis-Borok, suggesting that the environment at Volodya's department might be a good fit. The plan was that Andrei would get a permanent position there, but continue working with Gelfand in MSU as a part of collaboration with Volodya.

Andrei felt very impressed with how rigorous was his interview process at Volodya's department—as if he was not a graduate student interviewed for an entry-level job, but a prominent scientist seeking a leadership position. This made him realize how serious Volodya was about his team, how personal he felt about choosing and recruiting every new person, and he instantly felt he wanted to be a part of this team.

During his interview, Andrei met with several leading scientists in the department, followed by a personal interview with Volodya himself. It was late May, and the response from Volodya was surprising. "I would like to hire you as a junior researcher in my department," Volodya said, "but there is a complication. I have an open position right now, and I will lose it at the end of June. Can you finish all the paperwork by then?" The required "paperwork", as it turned out, included Andrei's formal resignation from his graduate school, and a reference letter signed by a full member of the Academy of Sciences of the USSR.

Andrei took on the challenge, even though he had no idea how he was going to be able to do all these things in such a short time. Academicians were a highly privileged caste, so that one could not easily gain access to them. Even Gelfand, a highly prominent mathematician, was only a corresponding member of the Academy, and thus not eligible to provide a reference and not even connected enough to guarantee one. The only standing Academician Andrei could even approach was P.S. Alexandrov—the head of the Mathematics division of MekhMat. At first Alexandrov refused flat-out, saying that he did not know Andrei enough to sign a reference. But eventually, through professional and even social connections, Alexandrov's signature was obtained.

It proved to be almost as difficult to process the dismissal from the graduate school. Summer was starting, and the officials in charge of the paperwork did not hurry to complete it. A few days before the deadline, Andrei realized that unless he did something drastic he would not be able to get his dismissal on time. He went into the office himself and took the papers, then walked them through all the essential offices. He finished everything just on time—on June 29, one day before the deadline.

In October of the same year Andrei successfully defended his Ph.D. and, after his degree had been approved by the State's Attestation Commission, was promoted within the department. Eventually, he became one of Volodya's closest colleagues.

Initially, Andrei did not spend much time at Volodya's institute, IPE. His project was pattern recognition in medicine, in collaboration with Gelfand at MSU. He visited IPE mostly for official duties, which, among other things, included trips to the vegetable storage base to help sort and store the harvested potatoes, onions, and other produce (a Soviet way of blending the society and ensuring that intellectuals contributed to the activities of the working classes). Andrei also attended regular IPE parties at Volodya's department, which included funny skits and songs staged by the department colleagues. Andrei never ceased to be amazed at the warm and family-like environment Volodya created around him, where people instantly bonded with each other and felt proud of their identity as a group.

Andrei's move to geophysics, and to a closer working relationship with Volodya, started in mid-70s, when F. Press and L. Knopoff came to Moscow to discuss the prediction of the possible location of strong earthquakes that Volodya led in collaboration with Gelfand and the geomorphologist E. Ranzman. Andrei was invited to these discussions by Gelfand, who led the mathematical part of the team. Andrei's task that ensued from this work became formalization of the morphostructural zoning of the Earth.

Andrei remembers this as happy and exciting times, filled with intense work, interesting discoveries, and the spirit of camaraderie only Volodya could inspire. Their institute was their life, and everyone in their circle cherished it.

He recalls a time when the director of IPE, M.A. Sadovsky, decided to visit one of the regular seminars in Keilis-Borok's department. Of course, he was so important that it was out of the question for him to travel to the location, away from his own department which was situated in a classified building in another part of Moscow. Instead, every member of Volodya's department had to get security clearance and a special permit, so that they could all travel to Sadovsky's office and hold their seminar.

Another memory is of a party at IPE, celebrating the 10th anniversary of the department. Someone brought alcohol, but it was technically against regulations to drink on the job, so everyone looked to Volodya for a decision. Volodya shrugged and said: "Working according to regulations is a form of a strike, and I would never want anyone here to look as if they were on strike." On the contrary, he suggested that to prove that they were not on strike they should absolutely have a drink.

Andrei remembers the building of MITPAN. Getting a building for the new institute was a nearly impossible task, and once they got it they had to be happy with whatever they could obtain. The building was old and required major repairs, and no one offered sufficient money, materials, or workers to complete the job. Volodya did not get swayed by this. He mobilized his team, the scientists, who worked on weekends and holidays to finish the construction. They all had to learn to do things they never expected they would have to. Andrei remembers spraying asbestos over the beams—a fire regulation at that time—with no mask or protective equipment.

After Volodya started traveling abroad, he spent extra effort to be able to share this privilege with his close colleagues. For some of them going abroad seemed nearly impossible in the Soviet times. Andrei would never have been allowed under normal circumstances, being single and from a Jewish family. Yet, with Volodya's help, he got to go, along with another close colleague Anatoly (Tolya) Levshin, an even more unlikely candidate (Tolya's daughter Olga had been married to the stepson of A. Sakharov, a famous physicist and dissident).

These were absolute red flags for the Soviet government, in constant fear of people with questionable background and political views or insufficient ties with Russia finding their way abroad. Volodya's department was full of people with such red flags in their dossiers, and he took it as a personal task to overcome these red flags, driven by his desire to do the best for his people. He created an intricate network of connections, gaining supporters at all levels of the government bureaucracy, Academy of Sciences, and the KGB. In many cases, he created these connections through befriending the personal secretaries of the officials. Andrei still remembers how they used to blossom with smiles and welcomes whenever Volodya walked into their offices, and gained him access inside, bypassing many important people in the waiting rooms. In other cases, Volodya connected with the officials themselves. He was very good in finding these ways, and people responded to him because, in addition to his need, they always felt his genuine interest. He was unlike anyone else they had to deal with.

Andrei's first trip abroad was Paris in 1978, with Tolya Levshin. In return each of them was requested to bring a separate suitcase of presents for the officials and KGB functionaries who helped them by not blocking their trip. This seemed like a bargain in exchange for the opportunity.

In 1980 Andrei went abroad again, this time to Italy. He spent some time in Bologna, where people still remembered how, 10 years ago, Keilis-Borok visited their institute and made them all work day and night.

Andrei once asked Volodya, when it was good time to call him. The answer was: "You can call me until 1 am tonight, and starting 4 am tomorrow morning". 3-hour night sleep probably was enough for him.

Voloyda was an avid reader of poetry and often cited lines from Shakespeare, from his favorite poet Boris Pasternak, or from his other favorite, musicals by Gilbert and Sullivan. He enjoyed music and theater, and often invited his colleagues, and well as international visitors, to exciting concerts and theatrical performances.

Volodya lived in a spacious three-room apartment in a condominium for people affiliated with the Academy of Sciences. The condominium was a set of three large buildings, aptly located on the intersection of the Dmitry Ulianov Street (named after the younger brother of Lenin, a physician) and Vavilov Street (named after a distinguished physicist). The only decorations on the walls were painting by Volodya's friend, the artist Yury Vasiliev. This apartment was a preferred gathering place for friends and visitors, and Volodya's wife Ludmila Nikolaevna (Lucia) Malinovskaya was known for her warm hospitality.

Andrei credits Volodya with introducing him to his wife, Amina. Amina lived in the same apartment building as Volodya, and was a friend of Lucia. Amina and Lucia often walked dogs together. It is possible that either Volodya, or Lucia, or both, might have thought how much in common Andrei and Amina had, so once, when the American scientist Allan Lichtman was visiting, Volodya invited both Andrei and Amina to dinner with Allan at his house. It worked even better than a simple introduction: after dinner, Allan had tickets to go to a concert, but he was so tired that he fell asleep, and Volodya offered the tickets to Andrei and Amina. They married very soon after that.

After Volodya developed close connections with the International Center for Theoretical Physics (ICTP) in Trieste, Andrei became a frequent participant in the annual workshops Volodya and his colleagues ran there. In 1990 Andrei went to Trieste with Amina and their two small children, and they stayed there for a year and a half. At that time, everyone who came from Moscow to visit Trieste told increasingly bad stories about the life back home. Listening to these stories, knowing that he was now responsible for his family, Andrei started thinking of moving abroad. He contacted L. Knopoff at UCLA, and D. Turcotte at Cornell, who found money to invite him for short-term visits. After negotiations, Andrei opted for a very low pay in exchange for a prolonged stay, and eventually spent almost two years as a visitor of the Geology Department at Cornell.

He knew by then that he wanted to live in America, but he did not want to create trouble for Volodya, who would surely encounter difficulties from the officials if it became known that he "allowed" one of his subordinates to defect from Russia. Fortunately, at that time the Soviet Union was disintegrating, and the restrictions were falling. Andrei returned from Trieste at the end of 1991, and in 1992 he received an invitation for a business trip to Cornell. He went there with a goal to stay.

In his efforts to find a permanent job, Andrei realized that the mathematical geophysics created by Keilis-Borok and his school was not that popular in the US, where geophysics was traditionally considered a part of Earth sciences rather than physics. Andrei realized that a more promising path for him would be to return to pure mathematics. He did, however, take advantage of his geophysics background in looking for a job, eventually getting a joint appointment in the Departments of Mathematics and Earth Sciences at Purdue University, where he works now.

Andrei's connections with Volodya remained active after his move to the US. They continued to visit each other and collaborated actively on earthquake prediction and modeling of seismicity. In 1998 Andrei invited Volodya to spend a semester at Purdue, securing joint support from the Dean, his own Department of Mathematics, and the Department of Civil Engineering, for this position.

At Purdue, Volodya and Andrei co-taught a course on earthquake dynamics. They also continued their work on earthquake prediction. Volodya received many visitors during this time. Once, his long-term collaborator Allan Lichtman brought Ms. Kay Goss, the deputy director of FEMA and a long-term member of Bill Clinton's campaign who knew of Volodya's and Allan's work on presidential elections and even informed Bill Clinton during his first presidential campaign that according to their article he was going to win. She came to Purdue specifically so that she could meet Volodya, and like many, was enchanted by him.

Volodya's health was already declining, especially his ability to walk. After he left Purdue, Andrei continued visiting him at UCLA.

Volodya and Andrei in 2001

He, and Ilya Zaliapin, one of Volodya's youngest colleagues, remained the closest to Volodya during these later years.

Some of Andrei's brightest memories of Volodya in his recent years relate to the way Volodya connected with people, causing strangers he had just met to instantly open up and tell him the entire stories of their lives. Once, Andrei took Volodya to a shoe store (a frequent activity after Volodya's feet became sore, even though he never bought anything). While waiting for Volodya to try on several pairs, Andrei watched the salesman who was helping him talk incessantly, telling Volodya about his problems with his girlfriend, health issues—personal things one would never normally tell to a stranger. Another time, Andrei and Volodya walked in Santa Monica and Volodya suggested to stop by a small restaurant that looked interesting. It didn't have a menu, so Volodya and Andrei went in and while they were waiting to be served, the owner came out, and the next thing they knew, he was telling Volodya the story of his life.

Andrei remembers how Volodya could instantly evoke this response in so many different people. It was part of his magic.

"In the Name of the Queen"

Anna Kashina:

From the time I first remember myself, Volodya has always been my best friend and favorite playmate. Whenever he visited us, I had his undivided attention. He visited often, and I cherished those times and looked forward to them.

Anna (Ania) and Volodya in early 1970s

One of our very first games: "the enchantress". Volodya was a stranded traveler, and I was an enchantress who miraculously appeared out of nowhere to solve all his problems. Thirsty? No problem, I will wave my magic wand and conjure a glass of water. Hungry? Here is a table full of food. Tired? Here is a castle you can spend the night in. We played this everywhere, at home and on the road. I don't remember how we stopped, but according to Volodya, one day I overheard him talking to my mother and telling her that this game was repetitive

121

and seemingly endless. He said it with fascination, amazed at the ways a child's mind worked, but as he spoke, he saw me listening. Since that day I never wanted to play this game again. I don't remember this episode, or any other reasons for stopping this game other than getting bored with it as I grew older, but I could never stop him from feeling intensely guilty. He felt guilty a lot when it came to me and my mother.

An early memory: I am coming back from a walk in the forest near our Moscow apartment, and see Volodya watching me out of our 8th floor window. I feel so excited: Volodya has come to visit! I start running. He leans out of the window and waves to me. In the essence of my child's joy, I yell to him: "Volodya, what did you bring for me today?" I still remember the feeling of certainty that he brought me something, and that I was going to love it. And this was of course not why I was so happy to see him. The real treat came afterwards, when I knew we were going to read books, tell stories, and play some interesting games. Just having him around made me feel

Ania and Volodya in 1991

happy, and this feeling stayed with me until his late years when I, alas, did not see him enough.

When I was six, he took me to a movie theater to watch "The Sounds of Music", which just came out in Russia. This movie became our favorite. Later on, I remember Volodya often taking out a newspaper with the lists of movies showing in Moscow and finding "The Sounds of Music" playing in some remote theater, then hopping onto the subway with me and going to see it. Sometimes we had to stand in the

122

street and ask for spare tickets when the movie was sold out. Surprisingly, we always got them. Later on, Volodya took me to watch a lot of shows using this method, when the tickets could not be found otherwise. Even though we must have watched "The Sounds of Music" several dozen times, I still enjoy it a lot.

He always read books and told stories to me. My favorite bedtime reading from very early on was the history of england, which he retold from Churchill's "History of the English-Speaking People". He made it sound so romantic. How Robert the Magnificent, the father of William the Conqueror, saw the beautiful Orletta washing clothes, and fell so much in love that he hoisted her up on his horse and swept her away to his castle in Normandy. How Richard the Lionheart, the brave and noble knight, led the crusades. How Henry the VIII courted each of his wives. These tales, which in reality were full of horrors, became a magical world we both shared.

Ania and Volodya in 1991 at the Hollywood Chinese Theater, looking at the signature of Julie Andrews

We liked to reenact some of the stories he read to me. I remember the big project around the "Golden Bug" by Edgar Allan Poe, which also involved some of my friends. We created maps and secret notes, writing them in milk and holding them to a candle to make the words

123

show. We buried the treasure in my grandparents' country house and searched for it using different clues. We even made a skull out of clay—or rather, for the lack of sufficient quantities of clay, two eye sockets, large enough to fit our improvised bug tied to a string. The bug was a real one, encased in a large plastic cube, borrowed from my other grandfather. The fun was endless, with every new book he read to me, and I so much looked forward to these games he invented.

Volodya rarely said "no" to me. His methods of discipline were far more subtle—and effective. Every time I asked if I could do something, he would pose the question back to me. "What do you think? Is it a good idea?" This felt more restrictive than a rejection. I always gave in to self-doubt and did not do these things—a very effective lesson in responsibility from very early on. I also strived on his approval, which meant so much to me, and learned to sense what would please or displease him. It mattered so much to see him happy and proud.

Once, Volodya, me, and my friend Fatima (we were both no older than seven) traveled to my other grandparents' country house and, for some reason, found very little food in storage and no help forthcoming in the next few days. There was a store, about 25 minute walk away, which was rarely open and sold only very basic things. Volodya assembled the two of us with a very serious face, and asked: "Tell me, what can you cook?" I said I could make tea. Fatima

Ania and Volodya in Borego Springs, CA in 1991: Volodya lay down to rest, and I (Ania) sat next to him talking about all the cactus needles on the ground. Eventually he jumped up—and sure enough, his back was covered with needles. I told him he looked like a hedgehog. We all laughed a lot. My parents took the picture.

claimed proficiency with scrambled eggs. Volodya nodded solemnly and pointed at each of us in turn: "You will be in charge of tea. And you will cook scrambled eggs. This should enable us to survive until help arrives." ("Help" was my other grandparents, who owned the place and could cook and run the household, and of course would bring a lot of food from Moscow). I don't remember if tea and eggs were really the only things we ate, and how long the situation lasted. We could always have taken the train back to Moscow, 40 km away, but it was so much fun for seven-year-olds to play this survival game.

Ever since I learned to use the phone by myself at the age of six, I talked to Volodya almost every day. This habit continued until he started having difficulty talking, in the middle of 2013. He usually picked up the phone with the words "Professor Keilis-Borok on the line!", pronounced in a cheerful voice with long rolling r's ("Prrrrofessor Keilis-Borrrok na prrrovode!"), and I always asked: "How did you know it was me?" and we laughed. He sometimes varied it with his other numerous titles (Laureate of the Soviet Ministry Prize for Construction, Academician Keilis-Borok, etc.). When he answered with a simple "hello" (which started to be his habit in the last couple of years), I knew he wasn't feeling well or something

Volodya with Ania and Ira in Louvre, June 1996

the last couple of years), I knew he wasn't feeling well or something was wrong.

In our conversations I could tell him anything at all, and I used these conversations a lot to relieve my stress and find good advice. No one else I knew understood me so well, and when he became too ill to talk and these conversations became impossible, it left a vacuum impossible to fill.

He often came to visit us, and we loved doing everything together. Later on, when we got our first VCR, we spent lots of time watching our favorite movies again and again. When more people were present, Volodya was famous for his ability to do several things at once. Typically, he could lie on the sofa reading a book, with TV on, simultaneously supporting conversations with several family members. When one of us missed something important on TV he could always tell us what it was, despite an apparent impossibility to have paid attention. By the end of the evening, he would also finish reading his book and relay its contents along with a verdict on its quality. This ability to multitask was so far beyond any of ours that all we could do was laugh.

When Volodya started traveling abroad, he brought me "The Hobbit" and "The Lord of the Rings" trilogy, and read them to me, translating into Russian from the page. The translation was not perfect, but it did not matter. The story was fun enough for both of us not to pay attention to the words. We also loved Sir Walter Scott, and read Ivanhoe, again and again, and later translated passages into English and back into Russian, laughing at the result. Our other favorites were "Quentin Durward" and, at some point, "The Talisman".

On one of his trips abroad, Billie and Frank Press introduced Volodya to Gilbert and Sullivan. Volodya fell in love with two of their most famous operas, "H.M.S. Pinnafore" and "The Pirates of Penzance". He tried to retell them to me, but only the "Pirates" had the story I found interesting. At that time, I was reading Rafael Sabatini's "Captain Blood", and pirates were very high on my list.

We both laughed about the scene where Gilbert and Sullivan's pirates defeat the policemen who came to arrest them, and then the police chief, lying tied up on the ground, tells the pirates that he is arresting them in the name of Queen Victoria. Which, naturally, makes the pirates release their captives and surrender, like any proper English pirates should do. The scene fascinated us so much, that, in combination with my interest in Sabatini, we decided to write a pirate novel of our own. Our challenge was to incorporate this scene into a Sabatini-like novel and to make it believable. Of course, we did not succeed, but came as close as we could with a scene where an eighteen-year-old court lady successfully orders the pirate fleet to attack a Spanish settlement "in the name of the Queen". This became the natural name for the novel (in Russian: "Imenem Korolevy").

The work on this novel took several years. We started with a very detailed outline of all the events, day by day, separating them into three story lines for the three main characters: Lady Anna—a close friend and lady-in-waiting to Queen Elizabeth of England, Richard Norton—a deposed young nobleman forced to become a pirate captain, and Sir Francis Drake—the commander of the pirate fleet in the Caribbean. Even though we both fiercely insisted that Lady Anna's name was based on Anne Boleyn, Queen Elizabeth's mother, and not on my name, when we wrote the novel we secretly assumed the roles of Lady Anna and Richard. I felt the same admiration from Volodya as the character in the book, and this was perhaps why the romance between Anna and Richard became purely intellectual, with no sensuality of any kind. Commercially speaking, this lack of sensuality became the novel's biggest shortcoming. It had everything else: internal logic, consistency, a dynamic eventful story, and a rich layer of historical facts that underlay every scene. The latter was of course thanks to Volodya.

We started writing this novel when I was in high school and finished it when I was an undergraduate student at the Moscow State University. Most of the writing was done during the trips Volodya took me on for every school holiday, as well as on weekends when he visited our home. I sat at the desk in my room and wrote in a notebook, and Volodya lay on my bed, surrounded by piles of books. Our discussions could get heated at times. Often we had to reenact the most difficult scenes, on paper or by actually standing up and moving around. Volodya remembered how whenever he got side-tracked I asked him "Are you working, or not?" I do remember teasing him a lot.

By the end of this work, I knew that I was going to be a writer.

This novel is laced with our personalities, our interactions, our memories. A small incident I recall: we were writing a scene where Lady Anna disguises herself as a serving girl and ventures into the city to meet Queen Elizabeth's secret agent. Trying to describe how she successfully escapes the guards posted at the doors to report on her whereabouts, Volodya started suggesting a phrase and then stopped, his face instantly going red. I asked: "What's wrong?" and he said, "I was about to suggest something completely indecent." I felt so intrigued. Indecent was the last thing I could imagine in connection to Volodya. I kept questioning him, until he finally revealed the "indecent" phrase: "The soldiers watched her attentively, but without any intention to discover her identity." This left me even more puzzled.

Ania and Volodya in 1994, Davis, CA

What was so indecent about this? After a lot more questioning, Volodya reluctantly explained that this type of attention would be directed at her figure, not at her face—a completely improper way to look at a woman. Back then I laughed, and eventually so did he. The phrase did find its way into the book.

We took special pride in creating our pen names. My name, Ann Porridge came naturally, a direct English translation of Anna Kashina. Volodya wanted to leave it at that, but I insisted on reflecting the fact that there were two authors. I did not want to take all the credit, even though I later learned that he had given this book to many of his friends saying that I wrote it myself. Under my pressure, we came up with "Sisters Porridge", aiming at an image of two old ladies writing romances rooted in English history. Volodya gave in at that point and suggested that his first name should be Vik (abbreviation of Vladimir Isaakovich Keilis-Borok), which was derived from his name but sounded sufficiently feminine. We both thought it was hilarious.

Volodya found a Russian publisher for this novel in 1996, when the end of the Soviet Union enabled the emergence of private enterprise. The book sold many copies, but predictably, Volodya never got paid. He kept a lot of copies, however, and carried them with him all his life, in addition to giving them to his friends and everyone he met who knew Russian. He always told them that this novel was written by his granddaughter, and I scolded him for it, but he only laughed.

"In the Name of the Queen" in Russian, cover by Olga and Sergey Karengin.

In the last weeks of Volodya's life, when he could no longer talk, I sat by his bedside whenever I visited and read him our novel out loud. I read it to him on the morning he passed away, and continued for about an hour after he stopped breathing. The words brought the comfort I needed so much, filled with his wisdom, his humor, his love. He put a lot of himself into this book, and it will always remain for me a memory of the happiest times in my life.

Art

Anna Kashina:

Volodya's love for science and his work always went side by side with his love of art. Poetry constituted an essential part of his existence. For many who knew him, his constant quotations of poetry—sometimes inappropriate or misunderstood, but always to the point—constituted a signature style of his interactions. These quotations, and the poems he took them from, had a deep meaning to him. Sometimes it became his way of dealing with life, when he found comfort and resonance in poetry, or sometimes—sound and rhythm that helped bring a necessary balance. To his last days he could recite more poems than me and my mother together, showing amazing knowledge of so many different poets. But his favorites, by far, were Pushkin and Pasternak.

Volodya always felt that those involved in creation of art are one step closer to the higher meaning of our existence, and he had deep respect and admiration for them. He supported his friend Volodya Barlas in his decision to quit his job in geology to become a literary critic. He was also very supportive of his other friend, the artist Yuri Vasiliev, who made a decision—dangerous in the Soviet times—to become an abstract artist. Among other things, this decision made it impossible for Yuri to earn money by his paintings, which were not considered a legitimate form of art in the Soviet Union, and Volodya helped a lot by buying these painting himself and introducing Yuri to many other admirers of his art.

Volodya was friends with the famous Russian poet Yevgeny Evtushenko, science fiction author Ivan Efremov, poet and author Bulat Okudzhava, and many others. When I was a child, I remember going to the studio of the famous artist Falk, shaking hands with the renowned pianists Svyatoslav Richter and Stanislav Neigauz, and of course visiting Yuri Vasiliev's studio many times.

During Volodya' s stay in Paris he became friends with the owner of the famous bookstore Shakespeare and Co., and attended the late-night gatherings of the literary and artistic Parisian boheme, often sleeping over on one of the couches in the store. In the US, Volodya became a friend with the science fiction author Poul Anderson, who introduced him to the Society for Creative Anachronisms and showed him some amazing historical recreations, including an exact replica of the Sherlock Holmes study on the top floor of one of the hotels in the San Francisco Union Square. Following Volodya to these places always felt like magic. I could never figure out how he managed to make these kinds of connections with people and discover such unusual things. His amazing gift of listening was likely the key.

Part of our home décor in Russia was a pastel drawing by the fa-

A trip with Yuri Vasiliev near Moscow, Russia.
Left to right: Sergei Kashin (Volodya's son-in-law), Ira (Volodya's daughter), Frank Press, Billie Press, Lucia, Yuri Vasiliev.

mous Georgian artist Lado Gudiashvili—a very elegant piece. The story of how it ended up in our home is one of such examples. Somehow, through one of his connections, Volodya once visited Gudiashvili's widow. Volodya knew that his favorite poet Boris Pasternak, in his later years, fell in love with a seventeen-year-old Georgian ballerina Chukurtma, Gudiashvili's niece, so he started asking the hostess what she knew about Pasternak. Learning of Volodya's fascination with the poet, Gudiashvili's widow said: "Oh, we have all the letters Pasternak wrote to Chukurtma. They are here, would you like to take them home and read them?"

Volodya told us later than his hands shook when he took the letters. It felt like the holiest of relics suddenly felt into his hold. He could not bring himself to take them home, or even read them, so the hostess, seeing his hesitation, offered him another gift: one of Gudiashvili's paintings. He wanted to refuse, but fortunately for us, took it at the end.

Academies of Sciences

Anna Kashina:

For a Soviet scientist, being elected into the Academy of Sciences meant stepping over into a higher plane of existence, joining the top of the Russian elite. Volodya, a Jew with highly unusual scientific background, working in a scientific field of his own creation—computational geophysics—could not possibly hope to ever become a member of the Soviet Academy of Sciences. Or so he believed.

When in 1969, soon after his move into the international arena with his work on seismic waves, he was notified that he had been elected into the American Academy of Arts and Sciences, his first re-

Volodya and his colleagues at the formal audience with the Pope John Paul II.

action was disbelief. Even more so, because the other elected members in that year were A. Sakharov and A. Solzhenitsyn, the famous dissidents and prominent political figures in addition to their background in science and art.

Volodya (left) shaking the hand of the Pope John Paul II, during a formal audience for the Pontifical Academy members. In the background: M. Marcelo Sánchez Sorondo, the Chancellor (left), and Prof. Nicola Cabibbo, the President of the Academy (right).

He expected trouble, but somewhat to his surprise nothing serious happened. On the contrary, three years later he also received a notification of his election into the National Academy of Sciences of the USA, a position of honor for scientists in the US and worldwide. People around him viewed it with a mixture of laughter and awe, that he would achieve this kind of recognition in America but not in his own country. Of course in Russia a typical academician at the time was an elderly patriarch, not a young energetic man who could speak so equally with people of many different ranks.

It took seventeen years for the Soviet Academy of Sciences to follow suit and elect Volodya one of its members. And here, an unthinkable happened: instead of the usual path of electing him a corresponding member and keeping him in this 'junior' status for a number of years, he was elected directly as a full standing member. Volodya told me later that there had been a whole strategy behind this highly unconventional move, staged by his supporters at the Academy and leading to such an unexpected success. I will always remember learning the news, on a late evening in December. Being a full academician meant a lot to his social status, the only honorable way in the old Soviet Union to elevate to the very top without selling your soul to the communist party. His election made us, his family, feel like royalty.

This election signified the next level in his international recognition which we often did not even learn about. In 1989 Volodya was elected a member of the Royal Astronomical Society in the UK. In 1992 he became a member of the Austrian Academy of Sciences. In 1994 he was elected into Pontifical Academy of Sciences in Vatican, a position that not only enabled him to be among the select few allowed into the mysterious and secluded Vatican City, but also entitled him to shake hands with the Pope and to be called "Your Excellency" within the Vatican walls.

Volodya felt very modest about these honors, telling everyone that he had been elected because of a "quota"

Volodya and Ira at a meeting of the National Academy of Sciences, USA, in Washington, D.C.

they had for Russian scientists, that he would never have been elected as an American member. It might have been true that being Russian helped him to get noticed, but it wasn't the whole truth, of course.

Traveling with Volodya to the annual meetings of the US National Academy of Sciences in Washington, DC, became one of the favorite things for my mother, and then also for me. Later on, Volodya also started taking me to the meetings of the Pontifical Academy of Sciences, and these trips created memories I would cherish for the rest of my life.

Volodya (center) receiving a degree of Doctor Honoris Causa from the Paris Institute of the Physics of the Earth.

Volodya shaking the hand of the Pope Benedict XVI. In the background: M. Marcelo Sánchez Sorondo, the Chancellor of the Pontifical Academy.

Italy

"You will regret every day you spend in Europe that is not in Venice."

—V. Keilis-Borok

Anna Kashina:

Of all the countries he visited, Volodya probably developed the most scientific and personal ties in America. But a close second was Italy—the home of his favorite Rennaissance art, the heritage of ancient Rome, and the romantic melancholy of Venice. Italy also was his major scientific base after he became first a frequent visitor and then the co-director of a biennial workshop at the International Center for Theorectical Physics (ICTP) in Trieste. During these visits he spent most of his free time in Venice, a 2-hour train ride away. He also visited Florence, the heart of Italian Rennaissance.

When Volodya was elected into the Pontifical Academy of Sciences in Vatican, a position he considered one of his highest lifetime honors, this election strengthened his ties with Italy and took them to a new level through his visits to Vatican and interactions with the world leading scientists from all countries on the topics related to the survival and prosperity of the mankind. He took his activities in Vatican very seriously, co-organizing working groups and focus sessions that in his view could seed the initiatives that would make the world a better place. Soon he became a member of the Council and served there for many years.

I was fortunate to accompany him on several of the Vatican trips between 2000 and 2004, and through these trips I shared a glimpse of the special feeling Volodya had for Italy. It became my favorite country too. Every night after the scientific sessions Volodya and I took a long way through the Vatican City, from Domus Sanctae Martae where we stayed, through Porto Santa Ana on the other end. The guards were tolerant to us as we strolled along the back side of the Basilica Saint Pietro, through the medieval part of the Vatican city that combined so harmoniously the old and the new, thousands of years of living history. We walked to Piazza Navona and sat at an outdoor table in one of the many cafes, ordering of *vino rosso caldo* (hot red wine), Volodya' s favorite that always left the waiters perplexed. We also walked through the city, until we got tired. The first time I saw the Roman forum was on one of these nighttime walks, and I will

never forget how it opened to me, from the top of the hill, highlighted by projectors—a magical sight. Volodya (who planned the route on purpose) watched my fascination and laughed, and it felt so special.

After our very first trip to Vatican, Volodya also took me to Venice. One of his Italian friends helped us to find a reasonably priced apartment for rent in the very center of Venice. We stayed there for a week, wandering around the streets, churches, museums, and far too many jewelry stores. It was so fun to walk on these streets with Volodya, discovering small passages, courtyards, streets so

Volodya taking a rest during our nightly walk from the Vatican to Piazza Navona. Rome, 2004

narrow one could touch the opposite walls with two hands, buildings that looked abandoned and decaying, eerily beautiful. I was stunned by Scuola San Rocco, and by the Venice ghetto where we came on a Friday night and ended up having Shabbath dinner with several dozen people we never met, just by walking into the open door of an attractive house. Volodya offered to pay for the meal, and the owner of the place was very offended. Later on Volodya reflected that he probably never should have.

Volodya in Italy

On that trip, my parents also joined us in Venice later on. Their flight was arriving early in the morning, and Volodya insisted on going to the airport to meet them because he was worried it would be hard for them to find us in Venice. He was 79 then and I was 34, supposedly the strong and capable one, but I simply could not bring myself to get up so early. Volodya told me to stay in bed and went to meet my parents alone, chuckling and saying "I am glad I am still good for something."

After Venice, we rented a car and drove together all the way to

Rome, stopping at Ravenna, Florence, Assissi, and visiting several smaller towns on the way. It was a magical trip, the last one when all our family spent such a happy time together.

***

Gabriella Poggi, International Centre for Theoretical Physics, Trieste:

The first time Prof. Keilis-Borok came to ICTP was upon invitation from Prof. Abuds Salam, founder of the ICTP. He was one of the Directors of the first Workshop on Pattern Recognition and Analysis

Volodya (front center) with the participants of a workshop in Trieste

of Seismicity in November 1983, what would be the first of many activities to come. In 1991 the "Structure and Nonlinear Dynamics of the Earth Group" (SAND) initiated. The group was established by Prof. Keilis-Borok and G. F. Panza and was divided in two main lines, Prof. Keilis-Borok led of the line of Non-Linear Dynamic of the Earth's Lithosphere. He worked together with the collaborators of his own institute, mathematical geophysics experts, Prof. Panza who led Structure of the Earth line, and other scientists who came from developing countries. We would see him at the ICTP as one of

144

V.I. Keilis-Borok and G.F. Panza during the workshop at the ICTP in 2009

the Directors of the Earthquake Prediction activities and in connection to the Group in the years to come. The advanced schools on nonlinear dynamics and earthquake prediction and schools on inverse problems in seismology alternated each year and through these he worked hard to spread his knowledge. He was very dedicated to his work and teachings which he took seriously, and along with the other directors and his team great effort was put in the planning and success of all activities. Prof. Keilis-Borok paid his last visit to the ICTP in October 2011. Till that day he was still active and made his way from one building to another, even if a little slower than back in 1983, but he was just as alert as he was back when he first visited.

During his visits to Trieste Prof. Keilis-Borok would also go to the Vatican in Rome, where he was a member of the Pontifical Academy of Sciences. Every trip also entailed a visit to Venice, a city he loved and every visit he brought a small gift for someone. He always

V.I. Keilis-Borok and K.R. Sreenivasan – a director of the ICTP in 2003-2009

allowed time for this and his gestures will long be remembered, not only was he an excellent scientist but also a very thoughtful person. Every trip to ICTP he would come to my office for a visit, that was always priority on his list, no work on his first visit, just a chat.

Prof. Keilis-Borok was highly respected and had become also a friend to many here. It is needless to say that his friendly visits will be more than missed.

***

Karim Aoudia, International Centre for Theoretical Physics, Trieste

Volodya for many years was a course director at ICTP and he led a research and educational program in non-linear dynamics of the lithosphere and prediction of extreme events. His contribution to ICTP and its community is invaluable.

The first time I met Volodya goes back to October 1996 and the last time, 15 years later, was in October 2011. Over these 15 years, I met Volodya once a year at he International Centre for Theoretical

Physics.

The first time I met him was in my first year of PhD. Volodya was always asking me questions and expecting answers. He had a very critical mind and high expectations... I will always remember his final statement after what was for me a long-lasting hour of questions and answers on "geometric incompatibilities in a fault system": "I think you should spend sometime in Purdue and go and work with Andrei Gabrielov." This was his rewarding statement (after a rigorous discussion) by which he meant to be encouraging, supportive and caring, spoken with his unique smile similar to the one you see in many of his pictures. Once you got to know him a bit more, there started the fun, with long discussions on politics and plenty of jokes! Science of course was his passion and his daily life when he was visiting ICTP.

As a scientist, I particularly appreciated Volodya's honesty and rigor in science and more specifically in earthquake prediction research. Volodya was for me a top-notch scientist and teacher as well as a wonderful Man. It was an honor to have known him.

And as Volodya would have said in the best of moods: "Shakespeare!"

Volodya on Piazza San Marco (Venice) during a flood

Israel

Anna Kashina:

Volodya always felt a special connection to Israel. Being Jewish meant a lot to him. More than that, he had relatives in Israel, and he did his best to keep in touch with them. While he did not travel to Israel often, he identified himself with this country in many ways.

From a 2003 article by Tom Tugend, Jerusalem Post:

"Quake Expert Eyes Israel as Forecasting Center.

The man hailed as the world's leading earthquake predictor, who has proven his mettle in California and Japan, now wants to help Israel become the forecasting center for the Middle East. ...

The Soviets granted him the privilege of traveling to Israel in the 1960s, where he organized two symposia, as well as to the United States.

Keilis-Borok is convinced that Israeli seismologists, geophysicists, and mathematicians have the 'Yiddishe kop' (Jewish brains) to build on his method and warn their country and the surrounding Arab nations of impending major quakes.

He urges his Israeli colleagues to 'shrei gevalt' (scream for help) to persuade their government to fund their work.

Seismologists consider the art of earthquake prediction as the holy grail of their craft, said Keilis-Borok. Many have claimed to have found it, only to be proven wrong, to the point that more than a few skeptical scientists believe the task may be impossible.

Not so, demurs Keilis-Borok...

'We have made a major breakthrough: discovering the possibility of making predictions months ahead of time, instead of years, as in previously known methods,' he said. 'This discovery culminates 20 years of multinational and interdisciplinary collaboration by a team of scientists from Russia, America, Western Europe, Japan, and Canada.'

...

He is not currently sounding any alarms for Israel, but he notes that large temblors have occurred in this area and along the Mediterranean coastline since biblical times. Going back into recent history, he has paid particular attention to the magnitude 7.3 Aqaba quake in 1995 and the 6.9 quake in Cyprus in 1996.

In both instances, all the prior symptoms pointed to major quakes. Keilis-Borok believes that, had his method had been developed in the early 1990s, he could have predicted both quakes a few months in advance.

He argues that better short-term quake forecasting is vitally important to Israel.

'Just as in war, Israel must be prepared because it has many unsafe buildings and because her enemies might take advantage of a devastating quake,' he said.

'There are excellent scientists in this field, especially at Ben-Gurion University, but also at the Weizmann Institute, Technion, and Hebrew University, but what they need now is government support.'

With such backing, he believes, Israel would become the forecasting center for the Middle East. 'The whole Arab world would either have to join Israel in this effort, or become dependent on Israel's preeminence.'

Keilis-Borok was born in 1921 and raised in 'a little Jewish section' of Moscow, near the Bolshoi Theater. His parents spoke Yiddish, but 'my Jewishness came from the intellectual atmosphere and the hunger for excellence,' he said.

By the early 1960s, his reputation was such that during the nuclear test ban negotiations in Geneva, both the Soviet Union and the United States relied on his expertise to help set the standards for distinguishing seismic signals emitted by an underground nuclear explosion from those triggered by an earthquake.

His service in Geneva and, later, his directorship of a Russian scientific institute, allowed him to travel widely, though he had to leave his family in Moscow.

Being Jewish, he said, 'created difficulties' but did not hinder his professional career, though it affected his daughter and granddaughter. 'The system was not a solid wall,' he said. 'It had lots of chinks, and if you weren't afraid, you could find the chinks.'

Such 'chinks' allowed him to protect and get exit visas for his young Jewish and other assistants, he said.

Keilis-Borok's 'tail wags the dog' mathematical method is now being applied to predictions in fields well beyond earthquakes. He and colleagues in other disciplines are into forecasting economic recessions, unemployment peaks, and surges in homicides."

***

Volodya's love for Israel also created common grounds for connecting with people, some of which became his long-term friends. Among them was Roald Hoffmann, a professor from Cornell, the 1981 Nobel laureate in chemistry. Roald, a remarkable scientist as well as a poet and playwright, fascinated Volodya, appealing to both his love for science and his love for art and those involved in creating it. Volodya and Roald connected very deeply and Volodya always admired him.

Here is what Roald wrote to me about their interactions.

"Your grandfather and I met some time in 1993, 20 years ago, in a meeting of a Committee of the National Academy of Sciences on, I think, some prospective cooperation on scientific journals with the

Russian Academy. Nina Fedoroff was also on that committee. When he realized that I had read Pasternak's poetry collection, 'Sestra moya, zhizn'', he began to quote some lines from it for me. And then we were off, with our mutual interest in literature, poetry in particular.

He was always so positive, so supportive. And never gave up trying to enlist me in his earthquake prediction research. I resisted."

When Volodya's colleagues celebrated his 90th birthday, Roald wrote a poem, "Constants of Motion", for the event.

Roald Hoffmann

CONSTANTS OF MOTION by Roald Hoffmann
For Volodya Keilis-Borok

In mechanics, a constant of motion is a quantity that is conserved throughout the motion, imposing in effect a constraint on the motion... Common examples include energy, linear momentum, angular momentum and the Laplace-Runge-Lenz vector (for inverse-square force laws). In quantum mechanics, an observable quantity Q will be a constant of motion if it commutes with the hamiltonian, H, and it does not itself depend explicitly on time.

Wikipedia

Classical

You've swung
so far as
to risk that
top trill of
your motion.
There, poised,
where beyond
would kill, you're
all potential.
To move. Again,
and when you
do, down, it's
all kinetic, and
what drew you
there compels
you rush on.
Don't stop, please.

Equations

No outer force,
the push/pull
of a father's
dream, career
jig. It's natural.
A caress given

a hug returned
Neither reward,
nor dissipation
figure much
in the meet
equations
of our motion.

Quantum

So the world
plays tough —
torn menisci,
nixed grant.
And then you
saunter by
with simple gifts
—
a touch, sweet
love. I am. But
now the test.
Imagine
it turned around:
We fall in love,
all settings "high,"
and then — in
just a trice

things fall apart,
shoes land, the
world turns on
its random wear
and tear. Where
are we, dear?

**Time rate
change**

Together, still.
But the equa-
tions,
heartless, say
stasis is not
an option.
Just move on,
kids, through war
bad knees, oh
a lost child.
To the parts
that cry and
muse, love is
the sole constant
of the motion.

UCLA

Anna Kashina (in consultation with William Newman and Joanne Knopoff):

Early ties: Leon Knopoff

Volodya's connection with UCLA started very early, when on one of his very first trips abroad he met Leon Knopoff. It happened at the IUGG meeting in Toronto in 1957. Volodya and Leon developed an immediate liking for each other. Scientifically, they found remarkable similarities in their work and ideas, but there was also more. Leon was a dynamic, creative man and Volodya felt an instant connection, finding Leon both very close in spirit and, at the same time, someone he admired. They had so much in common, both in their scientific research and in their love for music, art, mountaineering, and many

Volodya with Leon Knopoff

other things.

In the 1960s, the International Council of Scientific Unions (ICSU) organized the Upper Mantle Project, with ten working groups headed by the IUGG. Leon was one of the scientists in charge of this effort, and Volodya was chosen to head the working group on geophysical theory and computers. At that time, this combination was a novelty, but thanks to Volodya's efforts it became the most dynamic group, which has the most lasting effect in the field. As the result of this work, Volodya organized the Committee on Mathematical Geophysics, which has been meeting biennially since then. The first meeting of this committee was held in Moscow in 1964 and Leon was, of course, an honored attendee.

In 1971 Volodya convinced Frank Press and Leon Knopoff to take a trip to Garm, a geological station in Tajikistan, on the Russian side of the Tibet mountains. This geological station was established for monitoring seismic activity after a large and devastating earthquake in Tajikistan in 1949.

In Garm, Volodya showed Leon and Frank the data, which suggested a strong change in the ratio of the P-wave and S-wave velocities of seismic waves in the focal zone prior to an earthquake. This finding convinced the American scientists that earthquake prediction might indeed be possible. As a result, the US Congress approved a bill in 1975 that enabled the development of an earthquake prediction program. This was a major victory for Volodya's work that gained him recognition in the US and led to his special working connection with this country, including his Fairchild Scholarship from Caltech.

Volodya maintained strong ties with Leon throughout his life. their friendship and collaboration had always occupied a very special place in Volodya's life.

Member of the UCLA Faculty

In addition to Leon, Volodya formed very strong working connections with several other scientists at UCLA, including major collaborations with Michael Ghil, William Newman, and Michael Intrilligator. In 1998 his colleagues at the Institute of Geophysics and Planetary Physics (IGPP) and the Department of Earth and Space Sciences formally nominated him to serve as a University of California Regents Professor during the winter quarter, a highly distinguished position that enabled Volodya to establish a firmer base at UCLA.

This brought him into contact with many more UCLA faculty as well as research personnel and graduate students, especially through his offering a seminar focusing on his research contributions in earthquake prediction. The impact of his presence on campus led to an effort by UCLA faculty and administrators, through the Institute

Volodya giving a talk at UCLA

of Geophysics and Planetary Physics and the Department of Earth and Space Sciences, to create a permanent joint-appointment for him as Professor-in-Residence. He occupied this position from July of 1999 through February of 2010 when he formally retired and assumed Emeritus status.

While at UCLA, he continued to work with numerous co-investigators from the United States, Russia and other countries and contributed more than 20 papers on so-called predictability of critical transitions in complex systems, particularly on the dynamics of the lithosphere and predictability of geologic disasters. While a professor at UCLA, he taught seminar courses in seismology, in time-series and spectral analysis, and geocomplexity and earthquake prediction. His work was supported by a major grant from the James S. McDonnell Foundation.

Getting to Know Volodya, the Insightful Interdisciplinarian and the "Mensch"

Michael Ghil, ENS & UCLA:

M. Ghil with Volodya in 2001

A. First meeting, IUGG, Vienna, 1991

To the best of my recollection, I first met K-B—known to his friends as Volodya or, maybe to an even closer circle, as Velvel—at the IUGG meeting in Vienna, in July 1991. He was IUGG President at the time, and seemed to know of me, probably via Leon Knopoff. At the time, he was already aware of the importance that climate-related issues would take on in the near future, and volunteered a certain amount of support for my organizing a session at the upcoming meeting of the Committee on Mathematical Geophysics meeting in

159

1992. For some reason that I do not recall, it was not possible for me to take advantage of this support, but it already showed me both his scientific insight and personal kindness.

B. Marschak Colloquium, UCLA, 1998

As part of an effort to turn K-B's occasional visits to UCLA into a more permanent presence, Mike Intriligator invited him to give the prestigious Jacob Marschak Interdisciplinary Colloquium on Mathematics in the Behavioral Sciences. Volodya delivered the lecture—which had hosted several Nobel laureates and other luminaries—in February 1998. It was a captivating presentation on "Predicting Economic Recessions in the United States." [U.S. spelling, albeit illogical.] My wife, Michèle—a scholar in the Humanities and exposed to many presentations in diverse disciplines at the Ecole Normale Supérieure in Paris and New York University, where she had studied, as well as at the Alpbach, Austria, Congress Centre—declared without hesitation that it was the best science talk she had ever attended. It was also our opportunity to meet Anna Kashina, his granddaughter, and the editor of this book.

C. Sustainability Meeting at the Pontifical Academy, 1999

In March 1999, K-B organized a meeting at the Pontifical Academy of Sciences in Vatican City on "Science for Survival and Sustainable Development." Incidentally, he was at the time one of only two members in the field of Geosciences of the 120-member body. The other one was Nobel Laureate Paul Crutzen, a protestant. When I asked Volodya—himself Jewish, and very outspokenly so—what the rules on such matters were for an assembly of scholars hosted by a most catholic state, he told me that there were only two no-no's: one cannot be (i) a practicing atheist, i.e., one that actively preaches atheism; and (ii) a publicly known adulterer. The second item raised of course the well-known question in information theory about what exactly constitutes public knowledge.

Volodya chose the topic of the meeting at a time when questions of sustainability were still far from occupying as much attention as they have more recently. The setting of our talks and discussions—at the Casina Pio IV, built on the Vatican City grounds for the workings of the circle of friends of Galileo Galilei, before he fell out of Papal favor—was quite spectacular, and we were staying at the recently completed Domus Sanctae Martae, where the current Pope, Francis I, is living.

The outing of the meeting was a trip to Castel Gandolfo, the Popes' summer residence, currently occupied by the Pope-emeritus, Benedict XVI; it is a lovely cluster of buildings and gardens. On the bus trip from Vatican City to the Castelli Romani, Volodya and I were sitting together and started a conversation on possible scientific collaborations. I brought up his great talk at the Marschak Colloquium the year before and his interest in social-science questions. In his talk, Volodya had shown how to apply the pattern recognition algorithms that he and his MITPAN colleagues in Moscow had developed in the context of earthquake prediction to problems in the socio-economic sciences, such as economic recessions or presidential elections.

Some years before that, while still at the Courant Institute of Mathematical Sciences, I had developed, with two of my Ph.D. students there, a mathematical formalism for exploratory modeling of poorly understood and very partially observed phenomena. This formalism, called Boolean delay equations (BDEs), is a generalization of cellular automata in which the interaction times between the variables may depend on the pair of variables involved, rather than being the same for all pairs of variables. It seemed to me that—in addition to the pattern recognition algorithms that Volodya was already applying to socio-economic prediction problems—a very simple, time-dependent evolution model of BDE type could provide additional insights and help test existing prediction algorithms, as well as develop new ones. Formulating such a model would, naturally, have required interacting with experts in the socio-economic questions of interest.

Volodya's reply, after listening for a while to my suggestions, was, "Why don't we do this for earthquakes?" I responded that I had not realized so little was known about the latter as to justify such an idealized treatment. Be that as it may, this conversation was the starting point of our collaboration on applying BDEs to earthquake modeling and prediction, a collaboration that resulted in a two-part paper with Ilya Zaliapin, at the time a post-doc in the IGPP, as lead author; the paper was published in the Journal of Statistical Physics in 2003 (Zaliapin, Keilis-Borok and Ghil, 2003a,b). The proceedings of the 1999 Pontifical Academy meeting were published as a book, co-edited by K-B and the Chancellor of the Academy, Marcelo Sánchez Sorondo, in 2000.

D. Awards and Honors, 2004–2013

Himself a member of six or seven leading academies—including the already mentioned Pontifical one, the National Academy of Sciences, USA and the Russian Academy of Sciences—and awarded many other distinctions, K-B believed strongly in the importance of such matters, for the careers of those involved, and as a token of friendship between the nominator and the person receiving the honor. He was the nominator for one of my first major honors, the L.F. Richardson Medal of the EGU (2004), of which he had been the first recipient, in 1998. I participated, in turn, in several attempts to heap upon him some additional awards, but wasn't as successful, although he fully deserved them: it was our fault, not his.

In one of our conversations on such matters, Volodya told me: "You have to write in such a way as to make them feel that they will be honored by your sharing the membership (or award, or whatever)", or words to that effect. He certainly wasn't stingy with his praise. A UCLA colleague told me in confidence that he had compared some of my work with that of Jule G. Charney in geosciences and with that of A.N. Kolmogorov in mathematics, both of them certainly way out of my comfort zone.

E. Coda

These are but a few of my valuable memories of Volodya. The word "Mensch" in the title of this chapter is well understood by many non–Yiddish-speakers, like myself, throughout the Western world. It means, roughly speaking, a terrific guy or gal. I'm reproducing here part of the Wikipedia article for it:

Mensch (Yiddish: mentsh, cognate with German: Mensch "human being") means "a person of integrity and honor." The opposite of a "mensch" is an "unmensch" (meaning: an utterly unlikeable or unfriendly person). [A] "mensch" is "someone to admire and emulate, someone of noble character. The key to being 'a real mensch' is nothing less than character, rectitude, dignity, a sense of what is right, responsible, decorous." The term is used as a high compliment, expressing the rarity and value of that individual's qualities.

In Yiddish, mentsh roughly means "a good person." The word has migrated as a loanword into American English, where a mensch is a particularly good person, similar to a "stand-up guy," a person with the qualities one would hope for in a friend or trusted colleague.

That was certainly the way Volodya was, and the way he'd be happy and proud to be remembered. I found out, at a lunch we had in San Francisco—in the Yerba Buena Gardens near the Moscone Center, where the AGU was meeting—that his birthday at the end of July coincided with that of my late adoptive father. And I told him so, since it was a good way of expressing some of my feelings toward him.

Bibliography

1. Keilis-Borok, V. I., and M. Sánchez Sorondo (Eds.), 2000: *Science for Survival and Sustainable Development*, Scripta Varia 98, Pontifical Academy of Sciences, Vatican City.

2. Zaliapin, I., V. Keilis-Borok, and **M. Ghil**, 2003a: A Boolean delay equation model of colliding cascades. I: Multiple seismic

regimes. *J. Stat. Phys.*, **111**, 815–837.

3.   Zaliapin, I., V. Keilis-Borok, and **M. Ghil**, 2003b: A Boolean delay equation model of colliding cascades. II: Prediction of critical transitions. *J. Stat. Phys.*, **111**, 839–861.

The Turn of the Tide

From recollections by Ilya Zaliapin, colleague, University of Nevada:

Ilya started working with Volodya in Moscow and was the last scientist who ever worked under Volodya's direct supervision. After Volodya's move to UCLA, Ilya spent nearly 7 years there, between 1999 to 2006, first as a visiting scientist, then as a postdoc and full-time researcher.

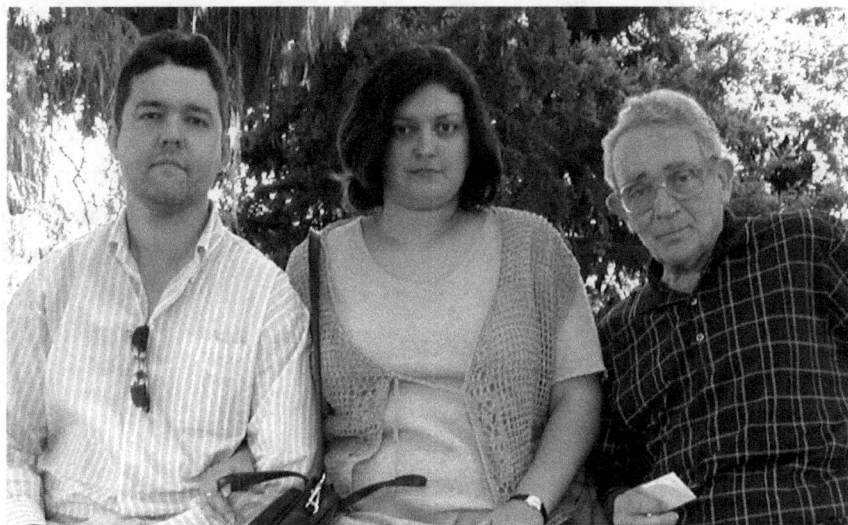

Volodya (right) with Ilya Zaliapin and his wife Elena in 2001

Like many of Volodya's handpicked colleagues, Ilya graduated from the Department of Mechanics and Mathematics at the Moscow State University. Ilya first came to MITPAN as a graduate student. At that time the Institute was quite big, and for a long time Ilya was working with senior colleagues —A. Lander, T. Kronrod, I. Rotwain,

165

I. Kuznetsov. Later he became a junior scientist in the laboratory of Vladilen Pisarenko, who was his PhD advisor. Only when it came close to his Ph. D. defense and the time came to decide on his future career was he introduced to Volodya for a formal interview.

Ilya still remembers this conversation vividly. Volodya started asking about Ilya's work, his interests, his skills. Shortly before that, Ilya had attended a seminar on application of mathematics to stock market analysis, and he brought it up in the conversation as one of his potential interests. Volodya frowned as he heard that. "Why stock market?" he asked. "Why not clouds in the sky?" Ilya chose to take the question seriously, and explained the difference, leaving Volodya impressed enough to accept Ilya into his group and initiate a project with him. This first project, on economic predictions, also involved I. Rotwain.

Volodya, who was 79 at that time, had a crisp and clear mind and was full of physical strength. Ilya remembers his first trip abroad, with Volodya, to ICTP in Trieste. When they were leaving, at the end of October, it was already very cold in Moscow, so they had to wear heavy, warm clothes. They flew in to Venice, and it was so warm and colorful, Ilya felt immediately dazed. Volodya said to him "I need to stop by to see my friends, then we'll go on to Trieste". He started walking, very fast, and in what felt to Ilya like a roundabout route. With his suitcase, in a heavy winter jacket, it was an effort for Ilya to keep up. Volodya, on the contrary, seemed not to be distracted at all by his luggage and winter wears and enjoyed the bridges, streets, piazzas, and palazzos of his favorite city.

Going places all around the world had a stimulating effect on him. Ilya recalls that often after a cross-continental trip Volodya would look very refreshed and more energetic than ever.

Volodya always seemed to have an infinite source of energy to keep everything in motion. Leading several large-scale research projects at his institute, writing new grant applications, actively participating in research (which involved sitting for hours and discussing data and figures), and generating ideas for new projects, he always found time to enjoy poetry, music, movies, or a long nature walk. His ability to handle multiple tasks and switch between different activities was truly remarkable, and remained so until his very last days. You could come to his office with any request (scientific or personal) at any time and be sure to be listened to and helped, as if the problem you were bringing in had the top priority on Volodya's list.

Ilya's and Volodya's first major project was the "colliding cascades" model, on which they work closely with Andrei Gabrielov and William Newman. The idea was to build a model that would reflect correct physical principles of material fracture and earthquake dynamics and be transparent enough to allow one to study in detail premonitory seismicity patterns. At that time their field was undergoing "nonlinear revolution", where many people were proposing nonlinear models and bringing in ideas from statistical physics and dynamical system theory. Volodya felt that theirs was a new model of that kind and was excited about it.

Volodya was a part of the Soviet scientific culture based around scientific schools and groups. He strongly believed in teamwork (although he would never use this word) and during his late years in the US he truly missed the team spirit that he used to enjoy (and create) during his years in Moscow. Compared to the closest members of Volodya's team Ilya started working with Volodya very late, and did it mostly abroad, hence he never was a part of the "core" group of Volodya's closest colleagues. However, he became probably the only one who mostly worked with Volodya directly one-on-one.

Ilya reflected that Volodya's unique style when working with people was to inflict a certainty that they were doing the most important thing in the world and no one else could possibly come any close to doing the same. He was not sure how Volodya maintained this feeling, but it stayed with and inspired Ilya the entire time they worked together. Only after he left Volodya did he realize that this feeling, whether or not it reflected the reality, originated from Volodya like some sort of a magic aura that enfolded everyone around him. Ilya believes that this was a major reason why Volodya was always able to assemble the best people into the teams working with him, attracting them by this magic he emanated. It was even more amazing because

Volodya never spoke in such terms, it just became a given to a person working by his side: "You are the best, working on the most important problem in the world that no one else could possibly do —and you are just about to solve it." This unique type of leadership called people to go —not after, but together with Volodya —to face and conquer new challenges.

Volodya was able to emanate the excitement and enthusiasm not only to his close colleagues deeply involved in research, but also in lay audience. Ilya recalls a public lecture at UCLA where Volodya was talking about prediction research in different systems (earthquakes, recessions, unemployment, elections). He was already in his 80s, which, together with his distinctively thick Russian accent, would not add to the vividness of the speech. Nevertheless, something had happened at that time and after the lecture he was surrounded by a large group of people who came for a chance of small talk, a chance to prolong the excitement they felt during the lecture. They behaved somewhat like sports or music fans, denying the necessity to depart with heir idol. A young lady with a humanity major was persisting in "doing joint research" and "continuing communications" and actually scribbled her phone on a napkin and pushed it into Volodya's hand. When later Ilya told about this to a senior colleague from the MIT-PAN, the person nodded seriously and said "Yes, I've seen that many times in the past... He is a sorcerer."

After Volodya got his position at UCLA, Ilya was visiting him for some time, and then eventually moved there, funded by a grant from James S. McDonnell foundation Volodya received. After finishing the colliding cascades model, they started collaboration with the UCLA professor Michael Ghil, developing a new idea of applications of Boolean Delay Equations (BDE) to Volodya's prediction models.

While at UCLA Ilya also witnessed and participated in Volodya's work with Peter Shebalin on a new generation of earthquake prediction algorithms. This work led to development of Volodya's final prediction algorithm: Reverse Tracing of Precursors (RTP). The initial application of RTP resulted in successful advance prediction of the Tokachi-Oki, Japan earthquake with magnitude 8.1 in 2003. Soon after, the algorithm issued an alarm for California —one that became the most publicized of all Volodya's predictions, and also, by an unfortunate coincidence, turned out to be false.

Volodya had mixed feelings about announcing the alarms issued by his team's prediction algorithms. On one hand, he wanted to share his predictions with as many professionals as possible, so that other scientists could evaluate his work. On the other hand, he realized that publicly announced predictions could cause panic and lead to harmful consequences in the society. He always hoped to find a safe way to disseminate the information to the disaster preparedness groups, enabling them to work on preventing major damage without causing general panic. In the meantime, he did what he always used to do: published the California prediction on his institute's password-protected web site and sent out the notification to a selected group of experts.

Although Volodya followed the usual routine and did not publicly promote this alarm, the forecast somehow leaked to the press and became widely publicized. It occupied front-page news in too many places, leading to TV interviews, articles, documentaries, and overall public hype. For better or for worse, this prediction seemed to become the cornerstone of Volodya's success. If the earthquake happened, everyone would finally believe him. If not, many would turn away.

While the public waited for the prediction outcome, Volodya used the time to widely promote the idea of earthquake prediction research within and outside the academy. The prediction failed. However, it was talked about so much that it pushed the turn of the tide of earthquake predictions in America. Together with this failure, Volodya's earlier successes were also drawn into the spotlight. While the public may not have felt it, many scientists started to realize more than before that Volodya's methods and his long-term goals have more merit than they were given credit for. Some continued his work. Overall, Ilya strongly feels that the story with California publicized prediction played an important role in shaping out the current global earthquake forecast research.

In his last years, Volodya worked with many people from different areas interested in predictions. These collaborations also involved prominent UCLA scientists, including Michael Ghil and the economics professor Michael Intrilligator. Ilya remembers people from the Los Angeles Department of Water and Power coming to talk to Volodya about possible response to future predictions, and Volodya's visits to the Los Angeles Police Department to collect the data on crime waves. He also remembers Voldoya's dream that never came to life: to bring a person in a uniform, a policeman or an emergency worker, to present at one of his scientific seminars. Volodya always felt that this alone could make people understand how important predictions were.

Ilya recalled some sayings that signified his interactions with Volodya during the years: "Advance prediction is the only way to test if science is correct," Volodya used to say. He also said: "The only value in our work is the way we can apply it. Without applications, there is no sense in doing what we do." And on interaction with people: "Each person is intricate, each has strengths and weaknesses, bright and dark sides. If you work with people, you should get the best out of everyone."

References:

Gabrielov, A., Zaliapin, I., Newman, W. I., & Keilis-Borok, V. I. (2000). Colliding cascades model for earthquake prediction. Geophysical Journal International, 143(2), 427-437.

Gabrielov, A., Keilis-Borok, V., Zaliapin, I., & Newman, W. I. (2000). Critical transitions in colliding cascades. Physical Review E, 62(1), 237.

Keilis-Borok, V., Shebalin, P., Gabrielov, A., & Turcotte, D. (2004). Reverse tracing of short-term earthquake precursors. Physics of the earth and planetary interiors, 145(1), 75-85.

Shebalin, P., Zaliapin, I., & Keilis-Borok, V. (2000). Premonitory raise of the earthquakes' correlation range: Lesser Antilles. Physics of the

Earth and Planetary Interiors, 122(3), 241-249.

Shebalin, P., Keilis-Borok, V., Gabrielov, A., Zaliapin, I., & Turcotte, D. (2006). Short-term earthquake prediction by reverse analysis of lithosphere dynamics. Tectonophysics, 413(1), 63-75.

Shebalin, P., Keilis-Borok, V., Zaliapin, I., Uyeda, S., Nagao, T., & Tsybin, N. (2004). Advance short-term prediction of the large Toka-chi-oki earthquake, September 25, 2003, M= 8.1 A case history. EARTH PLANETS AND SPACE, 56(8), 715-724.

Zaliapin, I., Keilis-Borok, V., & Ghil, M. (2003). A Boolean delay equation model of colliding cascades. Part I: Multiple seismic regimes. Journal of statistical physics, 111(3-4), 815-837.

Zaliapin, I., Keilis-Borok, V., & Ghil, M. (2003). A Boolean delay equation model of colliding cascades. Part II: Prediction of critical transitions. Journal of statistical physics, 111(3-4), 839-861.

Our Glorious Burden

Cleo Paskal, geopolitical analyst and writer, author of "Global Warring":

So, this is how I met Volodya. The conference shall remain nameless to protect the guilty. When I arrived, the preparatory session for speakers had already started. I slipped in quietly and sat against the wall. The convener, sitting at the head of a long conference table, was describing the plan for the next few days. Then panel leaders sitting around the table talked about their session. It was all a bit vague and muddled. My mind started to drift.

Then, suddenly, someone asked a question. And what a question. In a few quiet words, it undermined the whole concept of the conference and pierced the balloon of hot air that had been growing fat over the table. I stood up to see who had said the Emperor had no clothes. And there was Volodya.

The meeting staggered on, wounded but determined. It finally gave up the ghost, and people got up to leave. Volodya just sat there looking mildly annoyed. I went over and sat down next to him.

Cleo Paskal

"Bored?" I asked.

"Not anymore," he said.

And nor was I. Over the following few years —too few, as we only met when he was already in his 80s —Volodya taught me an incredible amount.

The lessons were short and intense, as I'd visit for only a few days or weeks at a time. But he still managed to teach me how to find simplicity in complexity, how to deal with bureaucracy, how to be loyal to your team, which Russian poems to learn by heart, how to look for yourself in the eyes of your great-grandchildren, the beauty of science, and the brutality of aging.

The lessons were difficult, stunning, touching, enraging, enlightening, but they were never boring. They have shaped me.

Some moments I'll never forget.

One night we met with a young scientist he had given a job to in Russia, and then helped to move to the US. The man hadn't become rich, or famous, but he had been given a chance to be himself. When he looked at Volodya you could see in his eyes a bond deeper than gratitude. And Volodya looked at him with warmth and pride. They had been through the wars together —loyal soldier and caring officer —and they had come out the other side alive. It was a short visit, but it was all either needed to show they still cared, and remembered.

My appendix had ruptured and been removed. I was recovering at home. Volodya called, worried. I hadn't been in touch in a while. He heard what had happened and became even more worried. What could he do? Knowing that if I cut the call short he would just worry more, and too tired to speak, I asked him to talk.

He started reciting Russian poetry he had learned by heart decades ago. And then he translated it verse by verse. Sometime he recited Shakespeare. Sometime a bit of Gilbert and Sullivan. He was, he joked, the very model of a modern major general.

The escape —to a world of stormy winters, heartbroken soldiers, epic battles and, very rarely, a touch of pure silliness, was the best medicine. After that anytime I was ill, or if I called and he was feeling low, he'd open up that corner of his mind again, start reciting, and we'd go back there, riding on dark horses through a snowy night, listening to the clash of swords, or the dripping of tears.

Volodya was never simple. One sentence could carry myriad layers of emotion and meaning, with hidden bear traps of humor and guilt. Once I was talking to Volodya on the phone. He had already complained that I hadn't visited recently, when I mentioned that my colleague was being a bit obstreperous. Volodya answered: "Want me to break his legs for hurting you? Or, better, come and break my legs, then at least I'll see you."

Volodya could be difficult to work with. His intensity could sear those closest to him. By the time we met, he had already refined his astounding work on prediction. Like him, it is brilliant, daring, innovative, complex, yet clear. He was burning to put it to work. But he was also wary of having his modern Delphic Oracle being misused. Having lived through some of the 20th century's greatest hardships, he deeply wanted to do something to prevent future suffering.

Volodya often talked about using his discoveries to "save the world", and he meant it. To me, that is where his urgency came from. Every time someone died in an earthquake that he thought could have been saved, he took it personally. He wanted to apply his approach to anything and everything. He had a secret that could save the world, and he wanted to use it. Now. It caused him to be impatient with the academicrats who attacked his name out of jealousy and blocked his work and his grants. And then to blame himself for getting impatient. As he got older, he blamed himself even more. He got angry with his body, with his voice, with his anger. With not having saved the world yet.

I don't know what will happen to Volodya's work. He taught me many things, and one of them is that you can believe you can make things better. And once you know that, you have to try. No matter the cost. Volodya tried. And it cost him. And those around him, especially his family. Now it is up to us to make it worth his and their sacrifice. Volodya, thank you for this glorious burden.

Last Years

"So many die long before their time...a constant reminder of injustice. But death happens not because of illness, accident, or crime. A man dies because he reaches the end of his life, the end of his strength, the end of his path..."

Vladimir Barlas

(from the poetry and essay collection "Life is Beautiful and Merciless" ("Zhizn' prekrasna i besposhchadna") by V. Barlas)

The Prayer:

(Volodya kept this in his papers, a typewritten document, probably third or fourth copy. Very likely one of his friends brought it to him, maybe Volodya asked for it at some point. The fact that he kept it all these years suggests that Volodya found this prayer of significance. Knowing him well, I can imagine that this is probably how he felt a lot of times, especially in his declining years):

"Dear God, give me the clarity of spirit so that I could come to terms with things I cannot fight, courage to fight everything I can, and wisdom to tell the former from the latter.

Dear God, you know better than I do that I am getting old and will soon become helpless. Keep me from the fatal habit of thinking that I must say something at every occasion on every topic. Hold me from my urge to improve everyone's life. Make me insightful but not boring; helpful but not dominant.

With the broad reserve of my wisdom it seems wasteful not to use all of it, but you know, dear God, that I want to keep at least a few friends until the end of my life.

Help me to keep my mind free from the endless trail of details, give me wings so that I could reach my goal. Seal my lips on the topics of illnesses and ailments. They are growing, and my desire to talk about them again and again is becoming sweeter with years. I do not dare to ask for mercy in sparing me the stories about the illnesses of others, but please help me, God, to bear them patiently.

I do not dare to ask You to improve my memory, but only to improve my humanity and humility in those cases where my memory clashes with that of others. Teach me a glorious lesson by showing me that I can also be wrong.

Keep me reasonably pleasant, I don't want to become a saint—some of them are so difficult to live with—but sour people are among the topmost creations of the Devil.

Give me the ability to see goodness in unexpected places, talents in people I don't expect to find; and give me, dear God, the mercy of telling them about it.

Amen."

(Prayer of middle-aged people, reprinted from "Morphology", 1962)

All his life, Volodya constantly questioned himself. In some of his papers I found allegories he created about himself: a likeable but overly submissive person who constantly invites abuse and cannot rest, day or night, until his brain itself becomes a scar; a brilliant sea captain who turns out to be a coward, leading his crew to their deaths. I found a recollection of an episode he witnessed as a 10-year-old child in one of the desolate post-revolutionary Russian villages: a dog, restless from hunger, running back again and again to chew on the same old bone. He compared himself to that dog. He also wrote down some comparisons of himself to a hunted rabbit, a sheep, or "an old lame horse that imagines itself a winged baby stag". All these allegories helped him to cope, but also signified the burden he carried all his life, until it became too heavy to bear.

It was so much harder on him in his last years, when he became truly lonely, with all his loyal colleagues and friends scattered around the world and his closest family living across continent. All this compounded with his inability to do the things he wanted to at work, which he bitterly realized.

Volodya never fully recovered from the wreckage that followed his failed earthquake prediction, which, for reasons unknown, had been so widely publicized. He continued his work at UCLA with admirable perseverance, never succumbing to public criticism and withdrawal of many of his colleagues and friends from active collaborations. Watching him, knowing how difficult it was for him, I always admired his courage, when he was willing to stand up alone to the whole world for the work that he believed in. But the strain of it took its toll. Volodya could never work the same way again.

Volodya with his colleagues in a cafe at Culver City, CA. Left to right: D. Ouzounov, V. Kossobokov, Volodya, A. Ismail-Zadeh; December 2012.

He was 84 at the time, and many took it as signs of old age, but it was not the case. His mind was as sharp as ever. He was full of ideas and felt he was one step away from perfecting his methods to the point where predictions of all kinds of things would become a reality. The problem was, in all his life he had never worked alone, always heading teams of experts, people who believed in him and were will-

177

ing to direct their unique expertise toward the common goal. And now, he found himself alone, with colleagues who were no longer willing to work under his supervision, with not even a personal assistant who could become his hands in working on a new project.

Volodya with his granddaughter and great-grandchildren on his 90th birthday (July 31, 2011). Left to right: Volodya, David, Anna, and Diana.

He often attributed his failures to losing personal charm. In truth, he was probably losing his ability to concentrate, but more than anything, he was losing his strength. We, his family, were too far away— on the East Coast and too busy to even see him often. His close friends, people who supported his move to the United States, people who helped his career since 1960s, were growing old, many of them had passed away. Even his students were not so young anymore. His institute was in Moscow, half a world away, and even there many of his older colleagues either moved away or were no longer active. He found himself truly alone. But he never gave up.

His last scientific talk he considered a success was in Athens, where he presented an overview of his lifetime work and was met with admiration and understanding. At that time, he started working on a book that would summarize his achievements. He was reluctant to do it, he preferred to spend his time on developing new predic-

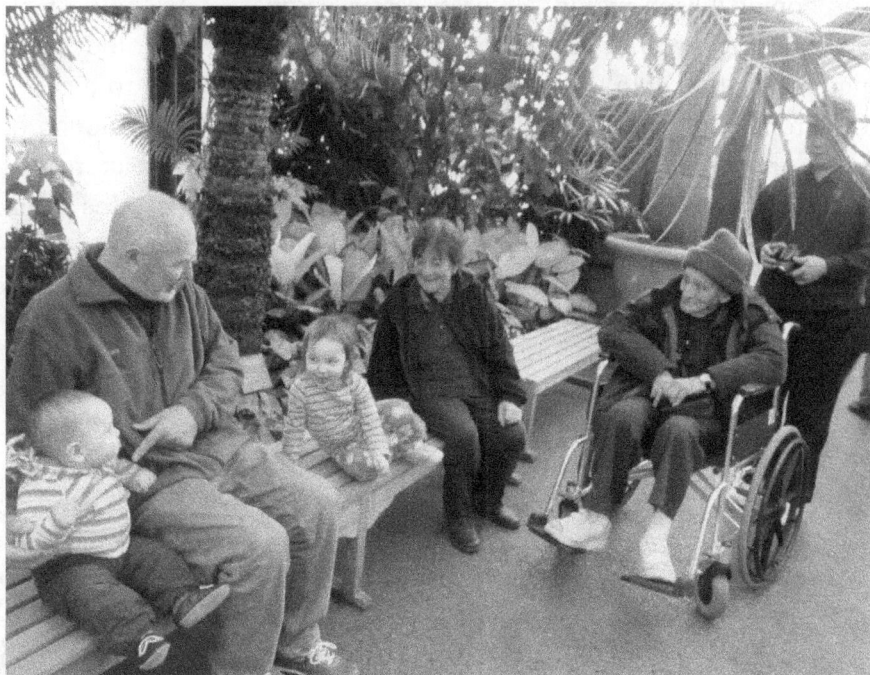

Volodya with his family in Longwood Gardens, PA, Christmas 2011. Left to right: David (great-grandson), Sergei (son-in-law), Diana (great-granddaughter), Irina (daughter), Volodya, Dawei (grandson-in-law). Photo by Anna Kashina.

tions and advance his science, but he also realized the necessity of it—and I, for one, kept pushing him. Still, without an assistant, with all his colleagues and collaborators far away, it seemed like a nearly impossible task to complete.

He started having difficulty walking. Watching him, my parents and I kept thinking of our last family trip to Italy in 2000, when Volodya was 79 and he could walk longer and faster than most of us. And then, in only a few short years, he could no longer walk without a cane, which was later replaced by a walker, and eventually, in 2012, a wheelchair. Still, he traveled easier than we did and always came to visit us in Philadelphia, at least twice a year.

In 2009 I had my daughter Diana, Volodya's first great-grandchild. He told me then that when she was born, his life changed, and he felt he achieved happiness he could never dream of. Since feeling guilty is in my genes, I felt so guilty for not doing it earlier. I was hoping Diana would catch at least a glimpse of Volodya at his best, to grow up with at least some of his involvement. Volodya told me then that he didn't think he could survive long enough to make it. Yet, from his few visits until the end of 2011, Diana saw enough of him to remember. She talks about him often, and drew pictures for him every time I went to visit him during the last few months of his life.

In 2011 Volodya's great-grandson David was born. Volodya was

Volodya with his caretakers at his retirement home in Culver City, CA celebrating his 92nd birthday (July 31, 2013). Left to right; Wilma, Gary's wife Belinda, Gary, Nancy.

so happy, even if more worried this time. I remember having a conversation with him when I was still pregnant. I was filled with concerns. How would another baby fit into our family? How would Diana take it that she is no longer the only one? How would she accept a baby brother? These worries seemed ridiculous to everyone else, but Volodya took me seriously. He said to me then: "When a new baby arrives, a new love is born." These words brought me so much comfort. And, of course, they were so true.

Volodya at his retirement home in Culver City, CA with his granddaughter Anna (left) and his friend Linda Pauling Kamb (right), July 31, 2013.

Volodya visited us twice after David's birth: first in the summer of 2011, to celebrate his 90th birthday, and then for Christmas the same year. That time, I had to hire a full time nurse to help him around. He went back early, and he was never able to travel again.

Being apart from Volodya during his last years will always be one of the biggest regrets of my life. He did not want to move to us for two reasons. First, he wanted to stay close to his office at UCLA. He came to work whenever he could, even when he had to travel in a wheelchair. The second reason was that he did not want to burden us. I still don't know how much each of these reasons factored in, but the UCLA connection prevented us from insisting on his move too much. Still, I tried to explain how much I loved him, how much I wanted him to be part of my life, but he was very firm.

His resolve not to burden us drove him to manage his own life even when we all felt he may no longer be able to do it—but he did so amazingly well. His ability to bond with people helped. As well as, of course, luck.

One of the nurses who came to help him when he still lived by himself was Gary Abrams, a remarkable man who had a long career as a registered nurse, and in his younger days also worked as a personal assistant to Norton Simon (the founder of Norton Simon Museum in Pasadena, CA). Volodya and Gary felt an instant connection to each other. As it happened, Gary was running a private assisted living facility for the elderly at his home in Culver City, and he offered Volodya to move in there. When it became absolutely clear that Volodya could not live on his own, he did that. It happened in 2010, Volodya was 89.

Gary became his lifeline, as close as family, not only to Volodya but to all of us. We did not meet Gary in person until 2013, but from the phone interactions, from the way Volodya spoke about him, we knew this was a person we could trust Volodya with. Gary's home became a home for Volodya, where everyone, including the nurses and caretakers, loved him.

When I visited Volodya at the end of July 2013 for his 92nd birthday, we held a party for Volodya with Gary, his family, and the staff at Volodya's home—I ordered food and Linda Pauling Kamb baked a cake. The next day, Volodya and I went shopping—I rolled him around in his wheelchair and we talked about books, about family, about life—just like we always did. We bought some toys for my children, which Volodya selected. It was a good day. And, neither of us realized back then that it was going to be our last shopping trip together. The next day he ended up in the hospital. Shortly after my visit he started losing his ability to talk.

I visited Volodya again in early September. He was bedridden, and taking him out for a walk was impossible, but he was alert when I came, and happy to see me. I arrived in the evening of September 3 and spent the evening with him before going back to my nearby hotel. On September 4 I sat with him all way and we talked a lot, even though I often had trouble understanding him. He even asked me to write down some of his ideas, but was not able to tell me anything coherent. He was disappointed when he looked at my page, where I was able to write only a few words: "organization, elucidated by...", "organization of the system". He smiled sadly. "Is this all I said?"

The next morning, September 5, his speech became clearer, almost normal. We had a good time, sitting and talking in his room. I felt then that he was going to get better. He quoted poetry to me, and even tried to sing a Russian romance song that I did not know. Then, after lunch, he went to sleep, and since that day he never spoke again. He never opened his eyes for long either. I went home in tears, and called him every day, asking a nurse to hold a phone to his ear so that I could tell him how much I loved him. I knew he was able to hear me, because he made sounds in return and the nurses told me he smiled and nodded sometimes. I only wished that during these conversations I could stop crying, or at least keep the tears out of my voice.

On October 17 Gary called me up and told me that Volodya stopped eating and drinking. I flew in on the morning of the 18th and sat with Volodya for the whole day, reading him our novel "In the Name of the Queen". He squeezed my hand, so I knew that he recognized me. He also tried to say something, but no sound came.

I planned to continue reading the next day, but when I came in the morning the nurses were playing one of his favorite movies, "My Fair Lady", so I decided to sit with him and wait until the movie was over. I sat by his side for about an hour. Then he stopped breathing. It happened around 9:30 am on the morning of October 19, 2013.

While Gary was making arrangements on the phone, I sat by Volodya's bed, reading aloud his favorite passages from our book. I knew he could no longer hear me. But I also felt it was the right thing to do.

The Cry
October 19, 2013

In the days after Volodya passed away, his family received many e-mails from his friends and colleagues, expressing their condolences and sharing some personal words. Many places published obituaries and wrote articles about him. We found great comfort in these words, from people we knew well, those we only heard about, and those we never met.

From the MITPAN obituary:

On the 19th of October 2013, on the 93rd year of his life, Academician Vladimir Keilis-Borok, the founder of the Institute, a distinguished Russian scientist, has passed away.

His exceptional humanity, scientific intuition, active style, ability to see the essence among a mass of factors, have enabled him numerous times to find and unite professionals from different scientific backgrounds around new, often as yet undefined, global tasks. In this way new areas of science were created—computational seismology and nonlinear dynamics in geophysics. Academician V. I. Keilis-Borok created the International Institute of Earthquake Prediction Theory and Mathematical Geophysics of the Academy of Sciences of the USSR (currently Institute of Earthquake Prediction Theory and Mathematical Geophysics of the Russian Academy of Sciences). During 1990-1998 he was the first director of this institute. He founded the annual publication "Computational Seismology", which has been published under his guidance since 1966.

One of the main signifying features of Vladimir Isaaakovich's scientific activity was sequential application of the modern computational and mathematical methods to the urgent problems in geology and geophysics. His first studies were dedicated to the modeling of the seismic source and the reconstruction of the movements within the earthquake focus from the observations. In his later work he developed the theory of propagation of surface waves in layered elastic media and obtained a series of fundamental results on spectral properties of seismic waves. These results underlay the development of the criteria for recognition of underground nuclear explosions, which remains the most efficient way of classifying of seismic events into underground explosions and earthquakes.

Vladimir Isaakovich focused his later scientific interests on solving inverse problems in seismology, for the first time defining them as a rigorous mathematical problem. Under his supervision new methods of modeling and defining the source mechanisms of earthquakes and reconstruction of the velocity structure of media from a combination of seismic observations were developed. These and many other works on direct and inverse problems in seismology served as a foundation of a new direction in geophysics— computational seismology.

The next key stage of Vladimir Isaakovich's scientific biography was evaluation of seismic risk and identification of the likely sites of strong earthquakes. As a result, a general probabilistic concept of seismic risk evaluation has been established, the task of forecasting of the sites of strong earthquakes was formally defined, and the relevant mathematical methods have been developed.

Vladimir Isaakovich's next task was to forecast not only the place but also the time of strong earthquakes. At the beginning his work was focused on identifying individual precursors of the upcoming earthquakes. At that time the precursor "an explosion of aftershocks" was formally defined, later its statistical significance was proven. Work on identification and statistical valuation of such precursors, carried out jointly with leading geophysicists from different countries, enabled the group to approach the task of developing the algorithms of mid-term prediction of strong earthquakes.

At the beginning of the 1980s Vladimir Isaakovich suggested a new approach to earthquake predictions, by shifting from individual precursors to a simultaneous analysis of a complex of characteristic features for each phase preceding a strong earthquake. This approach enabled creation of the first formal algorithms of mid-term earthquake predictions in the history of geophysics.

Lately Vladimir Isaakovich has been actively working on developing the general theory and methodology of prediction of critical events in non-linear chaotic systems. His results are important not only for developing of a new generation of earthquake prediction algorithms but also enabled development of algorithms for prediction of critical events in socio-economic systems.

In addition to his scientific work Vladimir Isaakovich is known for his multifaceted activities in development of international scientific collaborations. In 1992-97 he was a member of the Scientific Council of the International Association for the Promotion of Cooperation with Scientists from the New Independent States of the Former Soviet Union (INTAS), in 1987-93—a member of the Executive Board of the International Council for Science (ICSU), in 1987-91—the President of the International Union of Geodesy and Geophysics (IUGG), in 1979-83—the vice-president of International Association of Seismology and Physics of the Earth Interior (IASPEI), in 1964-79—the chairman of the Committee on Mathematical Geophysics. Vladimir Isaakovich organized many international conferences and symposia in Russia and abroad. He was the founder and director of the international school on nonlinear dynamics, seismic risk, and earthquake predictions held biannually at the Abdus Salam International Center for Theoretical Physics (Trieste, Italy). The thirteenth session of the school was personally directed by him in the fall of 2011.

Vladimir Isaakovich's outstanding achievements were recognized by his election into the Academy of Sciences of the USSR and a number of foreign academies, including American Academy of Arts and Sciences, National Academy of Sciences, USA, Royal Astronomical Society, Austrian Academy of Sciences, Pontifical Academy of Sciences, and Academia Europea. He was Doctor Honoris Causa of the Paris Institut de Physique du Globe and was awarded the L. F. Richardson's medal of the European Geophysical Society for his outstanding contributions to non-linear geophysics.

V.I. Keilis-Borok is the author of over 420 scientific papers. He personally trained 29 Ph.D. students and 15 Doctors of Science.

We will always cherish the memory of Vladimir Isaakovich Keilis-Borok, a brilliant scientist and a remarkable man.

Marcelo Sánchez Sorondo
The Chancellor
Prot. N. 0784 Vatican City, 21 October 2013
Vladimir Isaakovich Keilis-Borok (1921-2013)

'Give them eternal rest, O Lord, and may perpetual light shine on them for ever'

Dear Academician,

It is with deep sorrow and great sadness that we have to inform the Academic body of the death of Vladimir Isaakovich Keilis-Borok on 19 October 2013.

Born in Moscow (Russia) on 31 July 1921, in 1948, he received a Ph.D. in mathematical geophysics from the Academy of Sciences in Moscow, and was appointed to the Pontifical Academy of Sciences on 16 October 1994.

Prof. Keilis-Borok studied the dynamics and structure of solid Earth, with applications to earthquake prediction, the identification of nuclear explosions, and mineral exploration. Later on, his research was extended to the dynamics of chaotic and complex systems, with applications to the prediction of critical phenomena, socio-economic crises included. His team of researchers used new algorithmic methods for earthquake prediction. Keilis-Borok's method was retroactively applied to 31 cases dating back to 1989, with correlation 25 times (not including two near misses), including the Samoa area quake (September 2009) and the Sumatra quake (September 2009).

Keilis-Borok had also recently used some of his techniques to make socio-economic predictions with notable success. For example, in his work with Allan Lichtman, he used the mathematics of pattern recognition to correctly predict the popular vote winner of presidential elections in the United States from 1984 to 2008, as well as correctly predicting 128 out of 150 US mid-term Senatorial elections since 1986. He also applied this method to predicting rises in murder rates in Los Angeles, recessions, spikes in unemployment and terrorist attacks.

Prof. Keilis-Borok founded the International Institute of Earthquake Prediction Theory and Mathematical Geophysics in Moscow. He was elected to the American Academy of Arts and Sciences (1969), Austrian Academy of Sciences (1992), US National Academy Sciences (1971), Russian Academy of Sciences (1988), Academia Europaea (1999), and the Royal Astronomical Society (1989). He served as the President, International Union of Geodesy and Geophysics (1987-91). Vice President, International Association of Seismology and Physics of the Earth's Interior (1983-87), Board Member and Chair of Mathematics and Natural Sciences Section, International Council of Scientific Unions (1988-91), Founding Chairman, International Committee for Geophysical Theory and Computers (1964-79), and Expert, Technical Meetings on the Nuclear Test Ban Treaty (1960-90). He was also a member of the Committee for International Security and Disarmament, Russian Academy of Sciences (1998-2000); The Union's Scientific Committee for the UN Decade for Natural Disasters Reduction (1990-99); International Working Group on the Geological Safety of Nuclear Waste Depositories (1994-97). He was awarded the First Lewis Fry Richardson Medal for exceptional contributions to non-linear geophysics (1998), a Doctor *Honoris Causa*, Institute du Physique du Globe, Paris, and the 21st Century Collaborative Activity Award for Studying Complex Systems, McDonnell Foundation.

Vladimir I. Keilis-Borok was a Council Member from 1995 to

2004 and a regular participant in the Pontifical Academy of Sciences' activities, ever faithful in his dedication to our Institution's mission and always making a significant contribution to our Plenary Sessions.

The memory of his valuable contribution to the growth of the Academy will always be cherished.

Obituary: "Vladimir Keilis-Borok, 92, UCLA seismologist who predicted quakes"

by Stuart Wolpert, UCLA Newsroom, October 21, 2013

Vladimir Keilis-Borok, a UCLA seismologist and mathematical geophysicist who, along with his research team, developed a method intended to predict earthquakes months in advance, died Oct. 19 in Culver City, Calif., after a long illness. He was 92.

Keilis-Borok worked with other experts in pattern recognition, geodynamics, seismology, chaos theory, statistical physics and public safety to develop algorithms to detect precursory earthquake patterns.

In June 2003, the team predicted that an earthquake of magnitude 7 or higher would hit Japan in a region that included the island of Hokkaido by Dec. 28. On Sept. 25, approximately three months after it was predicted, a magnitude 8.1 quake struck Hokkaido.

"Earthquake prediction is called the Holy Grail of earthquake science and has been considered impossible by many scientists. It's not impossible," Keilis-Borok said in a UCLA press release issued in January 2004. At the time, he was a professor at the UCLA Institute of Geophysics and Planetary Physics and UCLA's Department of Earth and Space Sciences.

He also used his mathematical theories to accurately predict the winner of the popular vote in each U.S. presidential election from 1984 to 2008 and even applied his techniques to predict murder-rate trends in Los Angeles, recessions and the unemployment rate.

Keilis-Borok, who received his doctorate in mathematical geophysics from the Academy of Sciences in Moscow, began his career at UCLA in 1998 as a Regents' Professor. He retired from the faculty in 2010.

He was elected to membership in seven international academies of science, including the American Academy of Arts and Sciences (1969), the Austrian Academy of Sciences (1992), the U.S. National Academy Sciences (1971), the Pontifical Academy of Sciences (1994), the Russian Academy of Sciences (1988), Academia Europaea (1999) and the Royal Astronomical Society (1989).

He was awarded the inaugural Lewis Fry Richardson Medal by the European Geophysical Society for his exceptional contributions to non-linear geophysics. He was also founding director of the International Institute of Earthquake Prediction Theory and Mathematical Geophysics and served as president of the International Union of Geodesy and Geophysics from 1987 to 1991.

"Volodya," as he was known by those close to him, "will be remembered by his family, friends and colleagues around the world as a great man, scientist and teacher," said his friend Alik Ismail-Zadeh, a researcher at the Karlsruhe Institute of Technology in Germany.

"Beloved Professor, Remembered"

by Annie Lu, UCLA Daily Bruin

Vladimir Keilis-Borok, a professor emeritus in the UCLA Department of Earth and Space Sciences and an internationally known mathematical geophysicist and seismologist, died from a heart illness on Oct. 19 at his Culver City, Calif. home. He was 92.

Keilis-Borok is known for his contributions in the field of earthquake prediction and his passion to exchange ideas with different kinds of people, his friends said.

"He was much more than a grandfather," said Anna Kashina, Keilis-Borok's granddaughter and a professor at the University of Pennsylvania. "He was my best friend. He taught me how to be a writer, a scientist and a human being."

His research team had successfully predicted two large earthquakes that occurred in Japan and Central California in 2003, said Peter Shebalin, a professor at the Russian Academy of Sciences who worked with Keilis-Borok.

"He is one of the strongest leaders in the field of seismology," said Ilya Zaliapin, an associate professor at the University of Nevada, Reno who worked with Keilis-Borok on earthquake prediction.

Besides being an accomplished scientist in his field, Keilis-Borok was also known for his compassionate heart, said Kashina.

Friends of Keilis-Borok described him as someone who loved talking to all kinds of people, from young students to store clerks to waiters in restaurants.

They said he could immediately engage in inspirational conversations with people and was sincerely interested in what people were doing.

"He had an extraordinary ability to communicate with people," said Andrei Gabrielov, a professor at Purdue University who worked with Keilis-Borok. "I believe that's one of the reasons why he was such a great scientist."

Keilis-Borok had a distinguished career as a mathematical geophysicist in Moscow before he came to UCLA in 1998.

During the 1960s, he studied the problems of wave seismology. In the '80s he started working with a team of scientists on earthquake prediction algorithms, a relatively new area of study in the field of seismology during that time.

Keilis-Borok's main research focus at UCLA was an earthquake prediction method called "Reverse Tracing of Precursors" that can be used to predict the specific region and time of large earthquakes by examining patterns and precursors in reverse order.

Keilis-Borok's work in the field has made earthquake prediction a much more respectable discipline today when it was considered to be a controversial area of study by many scientists 10 years ago, said Shebalin, who developed the Reverse Tracing of Precursors algorithm with Keilis-Borok.

"People would criticize his methods for predicting earthquakes, but he was consistently optimistic about this field," Zaliapin said.

Besides studying earthquake patterns, Keilis-Borok also applied his method used to predict earthquakes to predict socioeconomic events with notable success, such as several presidential elections and surges in crime rates.

Among other areas of study that he was immersed in, Keilis-Borok had a special appreciation for Russian poetry and art, Shebalin said.

Shebalin said Keilis-Borok knew experts and specialists from all fields of study and loved discussing his ideas with young scientists and colleagues.

"He always told me that scientists should not work alone," Shebalin said. "He was extremely passionate with his work and always had a lot of ideas to discuss with different people."

Many remember Keilis-Borok as a person of passion and inspiration. He was known to have a warm and genuine smile that some of his friends described as "legendary."

Kashina said Keilis-Borok spent a lot of time reading and telling stories to her when she was a child. He had a special love for the mountains and often took her hiking and traveling. She said the times she spent with her grandfather later fed into her interest in writing and science.

"He taught me that there are a lot of things to learn in life," said Kashina.

Keilis-Borok is survived by a daughter, a granddaughter and two great-grandchildren.

John Vidale, Pacific Northwest Seismic Network:

He pushed the envelope on earthquake prediction. A lot of people had shied away from it because it failed in the '70s. He helped focus our interest on earthquake prediction.

Alik Ismail-Zadeh, IUGG Secretary General:

Dear IUGG Colleagues:

Today morning, 19 October 2013, Professor Vladimir Keilis-Borok, former President of IUGG (1987-1991), passed away at his home in Los Angeles, California, at the age of 92. He was a world-known mathematical geophysicist, who spent last three decades of his life to understand nonlinear processes in the Earth's lithosphere, which lead to earthquakes, and developed a distinguished group of experts in mathematical geophysicists who contributed together with him to the theory of earthquake predictions. There are not many scientists who consider that earthquakes can be predicted, but it was not the case of Volodya. He always told that "earthquakes can and should be predicted. It is a challenging task, but we should not give up. " Volodya liked to quote W. Churchill when he heard about concerns of his earthquake prediction: "This is not the beginning of the end, it's the end of the beginning".

Volodya's friend Frank Press (the Science Adviser to US President Jimmy Carter and former President of US National Academy of Sciences) wrote two years ago on the occasion of his 90th birthday: "Volodya, your career in science has been both creative and controversial - the same characterization that can be said of Fred Hoyle, Linus Pauling, even Albert Einstein. Knowing you, I am sure that age will be no impediment and that you will continue to put forward new concepts, that will stimulate much discussion, not only in geophysics but in the social sciences as well." Unfortunately, life is limited, and Volodya cannot anymore "put forward new concepts", but his students around the world. Volodya will be remembered by his family, friends, and colleagues as a great Man and Scientist.

Volodya Kossobokov, MITPAN:

The energy and spirit of Vladimir Isaakovich—a Free Man in an Evil Empire—were stimulating me from our very first meeting in January 1975 to the last one in May 2013 and, surely, will guide me for the rest of my life. I am one of lucky persons who shared time, research, and ideas with Volodya.

Frank Press, the Science Adviser to US President Jimmy Carter and former President of US National Academy of Sciences:

His passing leaves many people bereft. My family and I will never forget his kindness and concern, his warm and friendly ways, his knowledge and interest in all things. He had a special and unforgettable relationship with each one of us. We are all in mourning.

Paula Press, North Carolina, Chapel Hill:

I am so sad to hear the news of Volodya's passing. It's hard to imagine a world in which he doesn't exist. ... Memories of Volodya are interwoven in the fabric of my life and in that regard he remains vital, enriching and cherished.

Gabriella Poggi, ICTP, Trieste:

It is with very much sadness that I have learnt of Prof. Keilis-Borok's passing away.

I consider myself very fortunate to have met him, worked with him and have had many discussions over the years on a friendship basis. Not only was he a brilliant scientist but also a wonderful, considerate and very humane person. I will miss very much seeing him in Trieste. On his last visit to ICTP he called me to his room where he wanted to say goodbye because as he said it would be the last time we would see each other. We had a chat which I can now cherish.

It is difficult for me to accept he will not be walking into my office again. His presence however surrounds me, I have 3 large posters in my office that he bought me when he was in Venice after I had told him how unhappy in my new dark office. He walked in my office one day and said these are for you to brighten it up."

Efraim Laor, Israel:

I would like to offer our sincere condolences ... May it be comforted among the mourners of Zion and Jerusalem.

The departure of my Dear Bruder,.....Bleib gezund, Velvel was a very sad day for me and my family, who have been listeners for our endless loud Skype-conversations for 8 years. We truly feel the pain for the loss.

Giuliano Panza, University of Trieste, Italy:

KB passed away but he will remain among us with all he taught us, both as scientists and human beings. He finished to suffer a quite painful last part of his life, but we must be comforted by all the recognitions he received during his active life and for the school he was able to establish worldwide.

Uri Shamir, Technion, Israel, former President of IUGG:

I and my wife Yona personally mourn the passing of our dear friend Volodya Keilis-Borok. I was president of IAHS in 1991-1995 and hence member of the IUGG Bureau, while Helmut Moritz was President of IUGG and Volodya was Past-President. Over 3/4 of a bottle of Vodka, at a Bureau meeting in China, Volodya, with Helmut's support, tried to convince me to stand for election to the IUGG presidency. I was not able to undertake this onerous task at that time, so it was only in 2003 that I was elected to the post. In all the years of that period, and ever since, I remained in contact with Volodya. I admired him during the long years of our acquaintance and friendship, and was privileged to be on the mailing list of the Reverse Tracing of Precursors (RTP) project of earthquakes, in which a group led by Volodya attempted to predict months in advance the location and magnitude of earthquakes. Volodya was one of a kind: wise, soft spoken yet strong willed, he kept pushing for advancement of earthquake prediction - one of the toughest geophysical prediction tasks. The RTP project has been partially successful, albeit controversial, and I hope that it will continue in Volodya's spirit. The best move on, yet their spirit stays and motivated us to do our best. May he rest in peace.

Zhen Liu, Caltech:

I learned today from SCEC about the very sad news about Prof. Keilis-Borok. I have worked with him when I was a student at UCLA. His guidance and kindness have left lasting influence on my personal growth.

Renata Dmowska, Harvard University:

I will keep him forever in my mind as a fantastic scientist and great colleague.

Brendan Meade, Harvard University:

I just heard the very sad news about Professor Keilis-Borok. I never met Vladimir but I always found his work an inspiration and thoughtfully apart from so many madding fashions. During graduate school he once left me a note about block models on my desk at MIT. That someone like Vladimir would care enough to do this meant an awful lot to a young scientist. His determination to predict earthquakes is something that motivates me to try to make a difference.

Harish Gupta, President of IUGG:

It was about two years ago in December 2011 when I last met Volodya in San Francisco and we celebrated his 90th birthday with a dedicated symposium at the AGU Fall meeting. My association with Volodya dates back to early seventies when I met him for the first time during his visit to India. Over the past 40+ years, I was fortunate to have interacted with Volodya in different capacities. What Frank Press wrote about him two years back, sums it all about Volodya. May his soul rest in peace.

Raul Madariaga, ENS Paris, France

He did so many things for seismology, to get it out of the small circle of people dealing with seismograms and into a broader more physical view of seismicity. I will always remember him as one of favorite seismologists.

Karim Aoudia, Abdus Salam International Centre of Theoretical Physics, Trieste, Italy:

He was a top-notch scientist as well as a wonderful Man. Today he is on our first page of ICTP: http://www.ictp.it/about-ictp/media-centre/news/2013/10/in-memoriam-professor-vladimir-keilis-borok.aspx

---

Dimitar Ouzounov, Chapman University, CA:

I am keeping wonderful memories for VKB, since late 80's, when I was in IFS and also since last year, when we visited him at his residency in UCLA. I always will remember him as a saw him first—a very kind person, with brilliant smile and wonderful sense of humor. His powerful intelligence and visionary in science enabled him to be far ahead than others. Much more will come to understand fully the impact and legacy of his life. VKB will always be with us in our hearts and in our memories.

Peter Shebalin, Russian Academy of Sciences:

It is really difficult to accept this sad news. Vladimir Isaakovich really was not only our scientific guru, his erudition in literature, in music, in art made our joint work much more interesting and multilateral. He was one of the best representatives of intelligentsia we all hope to belong to. I know many people of very different ages and far from geophysics, all of them keep very warm memory of Vladimir Isaakovich. We all will keep him in our hearts.

Vincent Courtillot, former Director of IPGP, Member of French Academy of Sciences:

We all loved Volodya, a truly unique human being. Each one of us will miss him, and Institut de Physique du Globe de Paris (IPGP) as an institution of which he was a most distinguished doctor honors cause.

Helmut Moritz, University of Graz, Austria, former President of IUGG:

Volodya Keilis-Borok was one of my very closest friends. We were thinking along the same lines, and we could frequently communicate almost without words. He was not only a great scientist, but also a very deep person. I am profoundly sorry to miss him. If we had more of his kind, the world would be better.

Nafi Toksöz, Massachusetts Institute of Technology

My colleagues and I at MIT are deeply saddened by the passing of Professor Volodya Keilis-Borok. Volodya was a great scientist, good friend and distinguished mentor for many of us. Over the years, he spent many months at MIT lecturing and engaging in discussions about earthquakes and earthquake prediction. He helped inspire senior researchers, graduate students and undergraduates. His dedication to science, in general, and earthquake prediction, in particular, encouraged all those who were in contact with him. His passing is a great loss to all of us in the scientific community. He will be greatly missed.

Andy Michael, US Geological Survey:

I first met Keilis-Borok in 1978, at the end of my freshman year, when he visited Nafi Toksoz at MIT. Nafi had me testing one of Volodya's early forecasting methods based on swarms. Volodya was very encouraging and that started his long and positive impact on my career. He will be missed but undoubtedly his impact will continue to be strong.

Seiya Uyeda, Japan Academy of Sciences, Tokyo:

Volodya was a real pioneer who inspired us so much. I owe him tre-mendously. He was always so nice and sympathetic. I attach a picture with him. I am not sure about the dates and place ... We will remember him for a long time. Please pass my deep condolences to the bereaved family.

Ester Sztein, Board on International Scientific Organizations, The National Academies, Washington, D.C.:

Thank you very much for the heartfelt obituary for Volodya Keilis-Borok. I am sorry that I never got to meet him, but happy that I got to know him a bit through reading your piece. I am sorry for your loss.

Jerry Wasserburg, Caltech:

I have known Volodya in Moscow in the Soviet Union during my many visits there. Whenever I was there, as a member of a "dele-gatsy", he would always find a way through the security barrier to come in and visit and make arrangements to meet. His hospitality was always very large and included the family and you! I frequently was a guest in one of the family apartments. We knew him through to the end of the Cold War, the horror of Afghanistan (now repeated by my country the USA), through to the end of the Soviet Union, the start of the new Russia (now Putinized!) and all the experiences in the USA, including, very often with Leon & Joanne Knopoff at their home. Volodya's dedication to supporting young scientists back in Russia when he moved here was remarkable and successful. Our love of Volodya was, and will continues to be, very great. It was a true privilege to have known him, to know the family and to explore the new worlds he created wherever he was. A deep human spirit emanated from him and his willingness to go an extra million miles of effort to improve the world was a positive influence on me and many others. I remember when he and I were in a meeting in Hamburg, Germany. We went to a circus and got the notion to go into a trick structure where you had to find your way out. The walls were all mirrors in complicated arrangements. About 15 minutes inside, I lost my cool and could not find my way. I was, by that time frustrated and dizzy. Volodya figured a way out. When we got out, he said "Now, Jerya, let us, you and me, go away quietly, somewhere for two weeks and come up with a plan to save the world." We need him again, NOW! The greatest compliment that I ever got in my life came from Volodya after I gave a scientific talk at the Schmidt Institute that he had arranged. I cherish that to this day!

Joanne Knopoff, UCLA:

Dear Ania,

I send you and your parents and the rest of the family my sympathy and my warm thoughts. Volodya was a dear longtime friend of Leon's, and their friendship meant the world to both of them. They appreciated so much about each other—not just the scientific brilliance and their common scientific interests, but also the sense of humor, the love of the mountains, Volodya's discovery of and fondness for Gilbert and Sullivan, theorizing about the future of Israel and of Jews, and so much, no doubt, that I don't even know about that interested them both. They were an important part of each other's lives.

After Leon and Volodya had met, Leon soon grew to feel he could trust him, and asked him whether he could help with something that concerned Leon. Leon's parents had lost touch with an uncle of Leon's—his father's brother—in Leningrad during Stalin's reign. Leon's father had died when Leon was only 21, and Leon wanted very much to reestablish contact with his uncle, but he had only the pre-WWII address. All those years later he gave it to Volodya, thinking that Volodya would go through bureaucratic channels, but Volodya pursued the clue personally. One day when Leon went to his office at UCLA he found on his desk a letter from his uncle, whom Volodya had located. Leon was overjoyed and later was able to visit his uncle numerous times while going to scientific meetings. That meant so much to both of them.

Volodya was also very kind to our children, interested in them, and generous to them and to me. I remember the first time I met Volodya, at our home. He and Leon had been at a scientific meeting in Berkeley or San Francisco, and Volodya had come down to visit Leon at UCLA. It was in 1963, probably in August, for I remember that Katie was a baby sitting in a baby seat on the dining room table (she was born in mid-July of 1963), and we took a photo of her next to a big beautiful bouquet of roses that Volodya had brought for me. We have had in our living room since 1970 a charming set of 3 little chairs and a small table in Russian peasant-style lacquered wood that Volodya brought to us while we were on sabbatical in Venice, Italy, when Volodya came for an extended period to work with Leon. The furniture breaks down by unscrewing the legs, and Volodya had managed to bring it with him in one huge suitcase. We shipped it home as a precious possession at the end of our stay.

I am so glad that you were with Volodya at the end. Again, my sympathy and my thoughts are with you,

Warmly,

Jo

Joyce M. Somers, UCLA:

I had the pleasure of knowing [Volodya] for many, many years. I not only worked with him and Leon [Knopoff] but was fortunate enough to call him friend. He had so many interests that it would be hard to list them all: to my understanding he loved not only science but music (Gilbert and Sullivan was one of his favorites), poetry, literature, and Shakespeare. He taught many of us, so much about so many things, it would be hard to list here. He had a willing ear, to listen to my troubles. When I was joyous over the birth of grandchildren he shared my delight, when I lost two daughters his understanding and compassion buoyed me up. He was a man of all things...beyond compare.

———————————————

Brief Career Overview

Vladimir Kossobokov:

Over the years Prof. Vladimir I. Keilis-Borok kept working persistently on implementation of mathematical theories and computational methodologies into the practice of investigation of the solid Earth. Integrating the excellence of mathematical standards with vast seismological observations, he carried out major projects built upon a joint direct involvement of the world-class mathematicians and geophysicists.

Prof. Keilis-Borok developed new paradigms in the study of structure and dynamics of solid Earth, creating a theoretical base for a scientific prediction of geological critical phenomena. His pioneer understanding of the active lithosphere as a hierarchical nonlinear system has proved the existence of long-range interactions and has led to the design of reproducible earthquake prediction algorithms, which are based on identification and characterisation of the symptoms of near-critical states. He established crucial links between mathematical models of nonlinear systems and the analysis of observations of the real Earth, long before the ideas of deterministic chaos, pattern recognition etc. became fashionable. He is an early pioneer of the application of theoretical ideas from nonlinear systems to problems of practical importance, especially in the area of earthquake prediction, but also in the analysis of natural hazard assessment and in seismological inverse theory. The extreme breadth of his research and its applications is evidenced from his recent work on starquakes and socio-economic and political instabilities.

1940s—1950s: Theory of seismic surface waves, based on theory of operators; transition from point to finite models of an earthquake source; worldwide establishment of the region-specific patterns of earthquake source mechanisms.

1950s—early 1960s: Theoretical base for recognition of underground nuclear explosions; study of non-uniqueness in seismological inversion and development of methods to reduce it by joint inversion of different fields; development of maximal likelihood approach to computerisation of seismological survey.

1960s—1970s: Discovery of the first seismic pattern (later verified statistically as premonitory), reflecting the scaling and similarity of premonitory phenomena; introduction of pattern recognition of infrequent events in seismic data analysis; reconstruction of active fault systems and discovery of the specific structures around intersections of faults where strong earthquakes nucleate; systematic recognition of such structures in numerous regions worldwide (the recognition results are confirmed by the many occurrences of subsequent earthquakes); development of methodology, which integrates the data of seismology, tectonics, engineering, economy and demography, providing a probabilistic estimation of seismic risk in terms of damage to population and economy (numerous applications include estimation of seismic risk for mega cities worldwide).

1970s—1980s: Establishment of new paradigms in the dynamics of the lithosphere: long-range correlations, similarity and self-similarity, premonitory patterns in seismic activity; design of the algorithms for intermediate-term earthquake prediction; a theoretical modelling of new types of a stability break-up in the lithosphere due to rock-fluid interactions.

1980s—1990s: Introduction of concept of deterministic chaos in the dynamics of the lithosphere (earthquake prediction included); modelling the dynamics of tectonic block-and-fault systems and discovery of integral measures of instability of such systems; establishment of the two kinds of symptoms of critical transitions in the lithosphere: the "universal" ones, which are in common with other hierarchical non-linear systems, and the Earth-specific ones that depend on the geometry of the system of active faults; establishment of statistical significance of several earthquake prediction algorithms tested in real-time advance predictions worldwide.

In his later research Prof. Keilis-Borok continued integration of modelling and phenomenology in the study of critical transitions in chaotic systems of different origin. He led international research projects in USA, Russia, France, and Italy.

For his scientific excellence Prof. Keilis-Borok was elected to the American Academy of Arts and Sciences in 1969, to the US National Academy of Sciences in 1971, and to the Academy of Sciences of the USSR in 1987. In the following years he was elected to the Royal Astronomical Society (1989), the Austrian Academy of Sciences (1992), and the Pontifical Academy of Sciences (1994, Council member since 1995). In 1995 he was awarded the degree Doctor Honoris Causa, Institute de Physique du Globe, Paris. In 1998 the European Geophysical Society awarded Prof. V.I. Keilis-Borok with the first Lewis Fry Richardson Medal for research in non-linear geosciences.

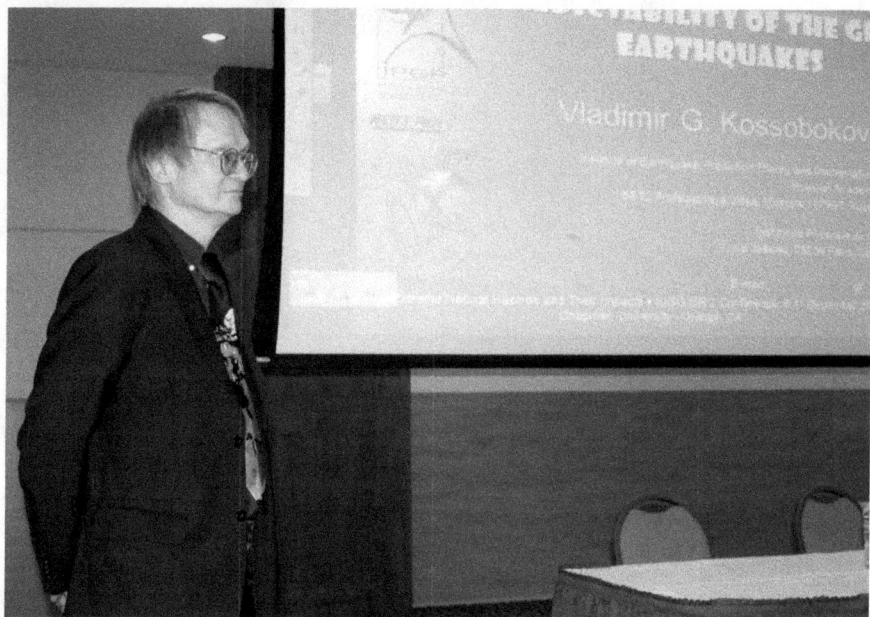

Vladimir Kossobokov giving a talk on earthquake predictions
December 2012

The Marvel of Keilis-Borok

Edited from the paper by Alexey V. Nikolaev, United Institute of Physics of the Earth, Russian Academy of Sciences

Written for Volodya's 80th birthday, July 31, 2001.

Vladimir Isaakovich Keilis-Borok occupied a special place in Russian and world geophysics. It is commonly said that a man carves a niche for himself among others in his field. Vladimir Isaakovich (V.I. for brevity) was carving out no such niche—he had created a niche of his own. Without him, that niche would have been nonexistent today. No one else would have worked for 60 years to create contemporary geophysics and to have done all V.I. has. This "Marvel of Keilis-Borok" is due to his own uniqueness, which manifests itself literally everywhere, both in the big and in the small.

Everybody acquainted with V.I. ended up in the field of his attraction or repulsion. So do I. I had known V.I. for more than 40 years, and my place was always destined to be somewhere outside his vast planetary system. Some things remained hidden from my view point, but other things were seen at a different angle, perhaps with greater clarity. Our personal contacts had been unsystematic, fragmentary; so will be my present account of him: my model of V.I. is incomplete, discontinuous, individual.

The greatness of a man of science is determined not only by his/her personal contribution to science (discoveries and research publications), but also by indirect influence through contacts, education, administrative activities, and more—by his spiritual aura. Keilis-Borok was a scientist to the core. He played the "center forward" in an aggressive "soccer" game over an extremely broad field. The lead-

209

ing line was established long ago and remains the same today: earth-quake prediction and seismic risk assessment. The method consists of a profound quantitative analysis of events and mathematical modeling of these events, with theory taking precedence over experiment. Both these features are reflected in the name of the institute he has estab-lished: International Institute of Earthquake Prediction Theory and Mathematical Geophysics (abbreviated to MITPAN).

V.I. had transformed seismology from a descriptive, almost geo-graphical discipline of the 1950s, into the contemporary physico-mathematical science of today. The exceptionality of V.I. lay not only in the fact that he, all by himself, determined new directions of re-search and put forward new methods for others to follow, but also in the powerful team he had created. This team was always driven by the spirits of solidarity, enthusiasm and creative freedom, stemming from the enormous, overpowering influence that V.I. exerted on his col-leagues.

The late 1950s to early 1960s, the time when this team began to form, were the beginning of a computer era. Computers were rare then, available only to select few. "Cybernetics", "computer", "algo-rithm", all these words sounded very romantic. Computerization of geophysics was a strategic goal of both Soviet and world science. This goal could only be attained by a young elite team headed by a strong adventurous leader.

Keilis-Borok undertook the computerization of geophysics, and this task determined both his own destiny and the destiny of his team—first a laboratory, then a department at the Institute of Physics of the Earth (IPE), and finally the International Institute of Earth-quake Prediction Theory and Mathematical Geophysics.

Computerization enveloped the whole world like an epidemic, shaping the face of geophysics, uniting it, and injecting new forces into international collaboration. During the 1960s, V.I. became the leader of the Soviet school of theoretical geophysicists and a world leader in this field.

As for myself, an outside observer, an experimental scientist, my breath was quite taken away by the seemingly boundless potential of computers. My awe extended not only to V.I. himself, but also to his "agents of influence", B.M. Naimark, V.F. Pisarenko, and A.L. Levshin. My interactions with them made me feel that high deeds could only be done by these "gods", that geophysics pivots on the probability theory, that geophysics without computers is no geophysics. I still remember the striking, showy assertions made by V.I.: "the new generation of computers will enable us to solve all problems arising in contemporary geophysics", "Naimark's spectral analysis program can solve 400 geophysical problems" (whence so many?), "computer analysis of seismograms will provide a complete solution to the problem of discriminating between earthquakes and underground nuclear explosions".

Academician M.A. Sadovskii, the director of our institute, did all he could to encourage young and ambitious scientists, especially V.I., whom he publicly called his favorite. It appeared that statements like this exasperated others who aspired to that coveted position, and M.A. Sadovskii could not help seeing it (that was the crux of the matter).

V.I. Keilis-Borok's department was rapidly developing and gathering strength. V.I. had always been of the opinion that mathematicians and physicists could advance any science; his team was strong indeed, but with a certain bias toward that particular side. In his paper "Seismology and logic" (1965) V.I. reported on the results achieved by his team ("25 mathematicians and physicists of the highest professional level") and discussed the state of the art in seismology, which was remaining unenviable in spite of all their efforts; he made the conclusion from that elevated vantage-ground that such must be seismology because it is so singularly abnormal. This issue seemed to have troubled him repeatedly: brilliant achievements in nuclear physics, mathematics, and biology on the one hand and, on the other, a slow-paced evolution of the old-fashioned and viscous seismology, which did not hurry to dent under the blows of logic. We were once talking about it in Garm, in the then-Soviet Central Asia, around 1960: why was seismology so "crude"—was it because its practitioners had low skills or because it was essentially refractory to any treatment? What could have been done in seismology if it was tackled by the best minds of contemporary physics and mathematics? V.I. was inclined to believe that the problem lay in the subject itself, in seismology. He seemed to find consolation in this. I was of a different opinion.

It seems to me now that V.I. had been in this internal debate with himself all his life, and had actually proven my case: thanks to his work and that of his disciples during several decades, seismology had assimilated contemporary advances in the theory of nonlinear dynamic systems, developed powerful techniques of mathematical modeling, made use of pattern recognition and classification techniques in application to earthquake predictions on the basis of seismological and geological-geographical data. A major victory had been won— seismology had found a way from an impasse into a revival.

It is said that the scientific level of a team is 90% that of its leader. As Napoleon once said, a flock of sheep led by a lion will beat a flock of lions led by a sheep (no offence meant for the MITPAN team). One exceptional feature of V.I. (apart from his strong and quick mind) was his charisma. The confidence he was radiating being carried away by a new idea, occasionally a wrong one (no matter), gained ascendancy over minds and hearts, young and old alike. His characteristic tones of voice and turns of expression were easily recognized in utterances of his associates; I first became aware of this in A.L. Levshin's talk, then in many others. It is in the nature of a normal person to wish to be governed by a stronger one. This explains why his team so excelled in solidarity.

It should be said that his was a choice team. Most of these people were brilliant experts in specific areas of mathematics, physics or geophysics. Each of these experts could be likened to a pure-bred dog with a long pedigree which had been bred to do something that it could do better than any other dog. To make a team of such diverse members (a "pack") takes a person who knows and excels in everything— only a good leader can achieve that. Undoubtedly, V.I. was one of the most brilliant examples of this human breed.

Each leader builds his relations with the team in his/her own manner. One, I. L. Nersesov, was an austere father, another, M.A. Sadovskii—an experienced and lenient (not toward everybody) general, still a third was a "Jewish mother". V.I. attributed himself to this third type. Such a leader had a huge advantage over the others for young scientists. However, later on, as researchers grew, this leadership style could potentially undermine their wish to follow their own path to independence—this was V.I.'s concern.

V.I. could be highly assertive. I had repeatedly observed it in his relations with other strong personalities and foreign colleagues. Speaking at a regular council of researchers held at the Institute of Physics of the Earth, he almost literally destroyed E. F. Savarenskii with withering but justified criticism. V.I.'s authority also extended abroad, where he was highly valued, loved, and respected. In 1983 I was elected vice-president of the IASPEI, V.I. being my predecessor. Once in his place, I was soon to feel caution toward myself on the part of the IASPEI Bureau; I was suspicious to them as a possible agent of V.I. As I now understand, he had become a nuisance during the 8 years of his work, thanks to numerous initiatives of his, most of them either beyond the scientific horizon of his colleagues or unacceptable for bureaucratic reasons.

When President of the IUGG, Keilis-Borok was active in bringing advanced branches of contemporary physics and mathematics into various research associations; his diplomacy was highly active and typically involved horizontal connections with other unions of mathematics and geology. He seems to have conducted that diplomacy in his somewhat brusque and cavalier manner. In 1994, V.I. and myself were taking part in meetings at the IUGG, he as the past president of the Union and I as the president of the IASPEI. The meetings were headed by the president of IUGG H. Moritz, who was an experienced administrator versed in principles of international diplomacy. I remember a meeting where he showed a quiet, soft-worded mastery to arrange a difficult situation. V.I. said to me: "Now I understand what a nuisance I had been when I was the president; in Moritz' place I easily could have destroyed friendships". If I remember it right, he compared himself with "a bull in a china shop". That was, of course, too searching a self-assessment.

Whatever the case, to achieve the marvel he did, to gain the fame of a world science leader, the head of an advanced research school, to get to the summit of science bureaucracy while not always showing himself a good diplomat, all this required a person of many remarkable qualities. One of these qualities, perhaps the crucial one, was independence of scientific thought.

Volodya (center) with A.V. Nikolaev (left) and his wife E.N. Sedova (right),
2000

Many years ago I put forward a nonlinear model of rock which is now termed the bimodal model. I asked G. I. Gurevich, the author of well-known rheologic rock models, to read my manuscript and I got a devastating rebuff. I was taken aback and went to V.I. to vent my grievance. "Alesha", said V.I., "You are still very young, a whole life lies before you. Never listen to anybody". These words were highly needed and important to me at the moment. I have retained this advice for life and always did my best to follow it.

V.I. was 40 years old then. Another 40 years have passed since. I am both glad and proud that he had always been very kindly disposed toward me. I have always felt deep respect toward Vladimir Isa-akovich, who is now a patriarch of science.

V. I. Keilis-Borok's Most Significant Publications

Compiled by Alexander A. Soloviev

1. Keilis-Borok, V.I., and T.B.Yanovskaya, Dependence of surface waves spectrum on a source depth within the Earth's crust. Izvestia AN SSSR. Geophysics, 1962, 11: 1533-1539 (in Russian).

2. Keilis-Borok, V.I. Computational methods of the study of the upper mantle. Vestnik Academii Nauk SSSR, 1964, 9: 88-89 (in Russian).

3. Keilis-Borok, V.I. Seismology and logics. In Solid Earth and Interface Phenomena. Washington, The M.I.T. Press, 1964: 61-79 (Research in Geophysics, Vol. 2).

4. Keilis-Borok, V.I., and L.N.Malinovskaya, One regularity in the occurrence of strong earthquakes. J. Geophys. Res., 1964, 69, 14: 3019-3024.

5. Keilis-Borok, V.I. Computational methods in geophysical investigations. Vestnik Academii Nauk SSSR, 1965, 12: 54-55 (in Russian).

6. Keilis-Borok, V.I., M.G.Neigauz, and G.V.Shkadinskaya, Application of the theory of eigenfunctions to the calculations of surface wave velocities. Review of Geophysics, 1965, 3, 1: 105-109.

7. Asbel,I.Ja., V.I.Keilis-Borok, and T.B.Yanovskaya, A technique of a joint interpretation of travel-time and amplitude-distance curves in the upper mantle studies. Geophys. J.R. Astr.Soc., 1966, 11, 1-2: 57-66.

8. Keilis-Borok, V.I., and T.B.Yanovskaya, Inverse problems of seismology (structural review). Geophys. J.R. Astr. Soc., 1967, 13: 223-234.

9. Keilis-Borok, V.I., Ye.V.Vilkovich, G.M.Molchan, Seismicity and principal seismic effects. Geophys. J.R. Astr.Soc., 1970, 21, 3-4: 323-335.

10. Keilis-Borok, V.I., The inverse problem of seismology. In Mantle and Core in Planetary Physics. Academic Press Inc., New York, 1971: 242-274.

11. Gelfand, I.M., Sh.I.Guberman, M.L.Izvekova, V.I.Keilis-Borok, and E.Ja.Ranzman, Criteria of high seismicity, determined by pattern recognition. In A.R.Ritsema (ed.), The Upper Mantle. Tectonophysics, 1972, 13 (1-4): 415-422.

12. Gelfand, I.M., Sh.A.Guberman, V.I.Keilis-Borok, L.Knopoff, F.Press, E.Ya.Ranzman, I.M.Rotwain, and A.M.Sadovsky, Pattern recognition applied to earthquake epicenters in California. Phys. Earth and Planet. Inter., 1976, 11: 227-283.

13. Caputo, M., P.Gasperini, V.I.Keilis-Borok, L.Marcelli, and I.M.Rotwain, Earthquake's swarms as forerunners of strong earthquakes in Italy. Annali di Geofisica, 1977, XXX, 3-4: 269-283.

14. Keilis-Borok, V., L.Knopoff, I.Rotwain, and T.Sidorenko, Bursts of seismicity as long-term precursors of strong earthquakes. J. Geophys. Res., 1980, 85, B2: 803-811.

15. Allen, C.R., V.I.Keilis-Borok, and L.Knopoff, Long-term premonitory seismicity patterns in Tibet and Himalayas. J. Geophys. Res., 1980, 85, B2: 813-820.

16. Keilis-Borok, V.I., and F.Press, On seismological applications of pattern recognition. In C.Allègre (ed.), Source Mechanism and Earthquake Prediction Applications, Paris, 1980: 51-60.

17. Keilis-Borok, V.I., L.Knopoff, and I.M.Rotwain, Bursts of aftershocks, long-term precursors of strong earthquakes. Nature, 1980, 283: 259-263.

18. Keilis-Borok, V.I., A worldwide test of three long-term premonitory seismicity patterns: a review. Tectonophysics, 1982, 85, 1/2: 47-60.

19. Barenblatt, G.I., V.I.Keilis-Borok, and A.S.Monin, Filtration model of earthquake sequence. Doklady Academii Nauk SSSR, 1983, 269, 4: 831-834 (in Russian).

20. Gabrielov, A.M., and V.I.Keilis-Borok, Patterns of stress corrosion: geometry of the principal stresses. PAGEOPH, 1983, 121, 3: 477-494.

21. Keilis-Borok, V.I., T.L.Kronrod, and G.M.Molchan, Seismic Risk for the Largest Cities of the World; Intensity VIII or More. The Geneva Papers on Risk and Insurance, 1984, 9 (№ 32): 255-277.

22. Keilis-Borok, V.I., L.Knopoff, I.M.Rotwain, and C.R.Allen, Intermediate-term prediction of occurrence times of strong earthquakes. Nature, 1988, 335, 6192: 690-694.

23. Keilis-Borok, V.I. The lithosphere of the Earth as a non-linear system with implications for earthquake prediction. Review of Geophysics, 1990, 28, 1: 19-34.

24. Keilis-Borok, V.I. Introduction: Non-linear systems in the problem of earthquake prediction. Phys. Earth Planet. Inter., 1990, 61, 1-2: 1-7.

25. Keilis-Borok, V.I., L.Knopoff, V.Kossobokov, and I.M.Rotwain, Intermediate-term prediction in advance of the Loma Prieta earthquake. Geophys. Res. Letters, 1990, 17, 9: 1461-1464.

26. Keilis-Borok, V.I., and V.G.Kossobokov, Premonitory activation of earthquake flow: algorithm M8. Phys. Earth Planet. Inter., 1990, 61, 1-2: 73-83.

27. Keilis-Borok, V.I., and V.G.Kossobokov, Times of increased probability of strong earthquakes (M ^{3} 7.5) diagnosed by algorithm M8 in Japan and adjacent territories. J. Geophys. Res., 1990, 95, B8: 12413-12422.

28. Keilis-Borok, V.I., and I.M.Rotwain, Diagnosis of Time of Increased Probability of strong earthquakes in different regions of the world: algorithm CN. Phys. Earth Planet. Inter., 1990, 61, 1-2: 57-72.

29. Kossobokov, V.G., V.I.Keilis-Borok, and S.W.Smith, Reduction of territorial uncertainty of earthquake forecasting. Phys. Earth Planet. Inter., 1990, 61, 1-2: R1-R4.

30. Kossobokov, V.G., V.I.Keilis-Borok, and S.W.Smith, Localization of intermediate-term earthquake prediction. J. Geophys. Res., 1990, 95: 19763-19772.

31. Kantorovich, L.V., and V.I. Keilis-Borok, Earthquake prediction and decision making: social, economic and civil protection aspects. In International Conference on Earthquake Prediction: State-of-the-Art, Strasbourg, France, 15-18 October 1991, Scientific-Technical Contributions, CSEM-EMSC, pp. 586-593.

32. Keilis-Borok, V.I., and A.J.Lichtman, The self-organization of American society in presidential and senatorial elections. In Yu.A.Kravtsov (ed.), Limits of Predictability, Springer-Verlag, Berlin-Heidelberg, 1993: 223-237.

33. Keilis-Borok, V. I., 1994. Symptoms of instability in a system of earthquake-prone faults. Physica D, 77 pp.193-199. doi:10.1016/0167-2789(94)90133-3

34. Gabrielov, A., Keilis-Borok, V., and Jackson, D., 1996. Geometric incompatibility in a fault system. Proc. Natl. Acad. Sci. USA, Vol.93, pp.3838-3842.

35. Keilis-Borok, V. I., 1996. Intermediate-term earthquake prediction. Proc. Natl. Acad. Sci. USA, Vol.93, pp.3748-3755.

36. Keilis-Borok, V.I. Non-seismological fields in earthquake prediction research. In Sir James Lighthill (ed.), A Critical Review of VAN, Singapore-New Jersey-London-Hong Kong: World Scientific, 1996: 357-372.

37. Keilis-Borok, V.I. On predictability of critical phenomena. Reflection on Science at the Dawn of the Third Millennium, Pontifical Academy of Sciences, 1997, 4: 111-128.

38. Rotwain, I., Keilis-Borok, V., and Botvina, L., 1997. Premonitory transformation of steel fracturing and seismicity, Physics of the Earth and Planetary Interiors, 101, pp.61-71. doi:10.1016/S0031-9201(96)03224-4

39. Keilis-Borok, V. I., 1999. What comes next in the dynamics of lithosphere and earthquake prediction?, Physics of the Earth and Planetary Interiors, 111, pp. 179-185. doi:10.1016/S0031-9201(98)00171-X

40. Kossobokov, V.G., V.I.Keilis-Borok, L.L.Romashkova, and J.H.Healy, Testing earthquake prediction algorithms: Statistically significant real-time prediction of the largest earthquakes in the Circum-Pacific, 1992-1997. Phys. Earth and Planet. Inter., 1999, 111, 3-4: 187-196.

41. Gabrielov, A., Keilis-Borok, V., Zaliapin, I., and Newman, W., 2000. Critical transitions in colliding cascades, Physical Review E, 62, pp. 237-249. doi:10.1103/PhysRevE.62.237

42. Gabrielov, A., Zaliapin I., Newman W., and Keilis-Borok, V., 2000. Colliding cascades model for earthquake prediction, Geophysical Journal International, 143, pp. 427-437. doi:10.1046/j.1365-246X.2000.01237.x

43. Keilis-Borok, V.I. Colliding cascades: a model for prediction of critical transitions. In Science and the Future of Mankind. Science for Man and Man for Science. The Proceedings of the Preparatory Session, 12-14 November 1999, and the Jubilee Plenary Session, 10-13 November 2000. Pontificiae Academiae Scientiarvm Scripta Varia, Vatican City, 2001, pp. 408-425.

44. Keilis-Borok, V., J.H.Stock, A.Soloviev, and P.Mikhalev, Prerecession pattern of six economic indicators in the USA. Journal of Forecasting, 2000, 19, 1: 65-80.

45. Kossobokov, V.G., Keilis-Borok, V.I., and Baolian Cheng, 2000. Similarities of multiple fracturing on a neutron star and on the Earth. Physical Review E, Vol.61, N4, pp.3529-3533. doi:10.1103/PhysRevE.61.3529

46. Keilis-Borok, V., Ismail-Zadeh, A., Kossobokov, V., and Shebalin, P., 2001. Non-linear dynamics of the lithosphere and intermediate-term earthquake prediction, Tectonophysics, 338, pp. 247-260. doi:10.1016/S0040-1951(01)00080-4

47. Keilis-Borok, V.I. Earthquake prediction: State-of-the-art and emerging possibilities. Annu. Rev. Earth Planet Sci., 2002, 30: 1-33. doi:10.1146/annurev.earth.30.100301.083856

48. Keilis-Borok, V.I. Basic science for prediction and reduction of geological disasters. In T.Beer and A.Ismail-Zadeh (eds), Risk Science and Sustainability. Kluwer Academic Publishers, Dordrecht-Boston-London, 2003, pp. 29-38 (NATO Science Series. II. Mathematics, Physics and Chemistry – Vol. 112).

49. Keilis-Borok, V.I., D.J.Gascon, A.A.Soloviev, M.D.Intriligator, R.Pichardo, and F.E.Winberg, On predictability of homicide surges in megacities. In T.Beer and A.Ismail-Zadeh (eds), Risk Science and Sustainability. Kluwer Academic Publishers, Dordrecht-Boston-London, 2003, pp. 91-110 (NATO Science Series. II. Mathematics, Physics and Chemistry – Vol. 112).

50. Keilis-Borok, V.I., D.J.Gascon, A.A.Soloviev, M.D.Intriligator, R.Pichardo, and F.E.Winberg, On the predictability of crime waves in megacities – extended summary. In The Caltural Values of Science. Plenary Session, 8-11 November 2002. Pontificiae Academiae Scientiarvm Scripta Varia, 105, Vatican City, 2003, pp. 221-229.

51. Jin, A., K.Aki, Z.Liu, and V.Keilis-Borok, Seismological evidence for the brittle-ductile interaction hypothesis on earthquake loading. Earth Planets Space, 2004, 56: 823-830.

52. Keilis-Borok, V., P.Shebalin, A.Gabrielov, and D.Turcotte, Reverse tracing of short-term earthquake precursors. Phys. Earth and Planet. Inter., 2004, 145, 1-4: 75-85.

53. Shebalin, P., V.Keilis-Borok, I.Zaliapin, S.Uyeda, T.Nagao, and N.Tsybin, Advance short-term prediction of the large Tokachi-oki earthquake, September 25, 2003, M = 8.1. A case history. Earth, Planets and Space, 2004, 56, 8: 715-724.

54. Keilis-Borok, V.I., A.A.Soloviev, C.B.Allègre, A.N.Sobolevskii, and M.D.Intriligator, Patterns of macroeconomic indicators preceding the unemployment rise in Western Europe and the USA, Pattern Recognition, 2005, 38, 3: 423-435.

55. Zaliapin, I., A.Jin, Z.Lui, K.Aki, and V.Keilis-Borok, Temporal (un)correlations between coda Q-1 and seismicity – Multiscale Trend Analysis. Pure and Appl. Geophys., 2005, 162: 827-841.

56. Shebalin, P., V.Keilis-Borok, A.Gabrielov, I.Zaliapin, and D.Turcotte, Short-term earthquake prediction by reverse analysis of lithosphere dynamics. Tectonophysics, 2006, 413: 63-75.

57. Keilis-Borok, V.I., A.A.Soloviev, M.D.Intriligator, and F.E.Winberg, Pattern of macroeconomic indicators preceding the end of an American economic recession. J. Pattern Recognition Res., 2008, 3, 1: 40-53.

58. Molchan, G., and V.Keilis-Borok, Earthquake prediction: probabilistic aspect. Geophys. J. Int., 2008, 173, 3: 1012–1017.

59. Gabrielov, A., V.Keilis-Borok, Ya.Sinai, and I.Zaliapin, Statistical properties of the cluster dynamics of the systems of statistical mechanics. In G.Gallavotti, W.L.Reiter, and J.Yngvason (eds.), Boltzmann's Legacy. European Mathematical Society, Zurich, 2008, pp. 203-215 (ESI Lectures in Mathematics and Physics).

60. Keilis-Borok, V.I., A.Soloviev, A.Gabrielov, and I.Zaliapin, Change of scaling before extreme events in complex systems. In W.Arber, N.Cabibbo, and M.S.Sorondo (eds), Predictability in Science: Accuracy and Limitations. The Proceedings of the Plenary Session 3-6 November 2006. Pontificia Academia Scientiarvm, Vatican City, 2008, pp. 37-45, 240 (Pontificia Academia Scientiarvm, Acta 19).

61. Keilis-Borok, V., A.Gabrielov, and A.Soloviev, Geo-complexity and earthquake prediction. In: Meyers R. (ed.) Encyclopedia of Complexity and Systems Science, Springer, New York, 2009, pp. 4178-4194. doi: 10.1007/978-0387-30440-3_246

62. Keilis-Borok, V., A.Soloviev, and A.Lichtman, Extreme events in socio-economic and political complex systems, predictability of. In: Meyers R. (ed.) Encyclopedia of Complexity and Systems Science, Springer, New York, 2009, pp. 3300-3317. doi: 10.1007/978-0387-30440-3_196

63. Davis, C.A., V.Keilis-Borok, G.Molchan, P.Shebalin, P.Lahr, and C.Plumb, Earthquake prediction and disaster preparedness: Interactive analysis. Natural Hazards Review, ASCE, 2010, 11, 4: 173-184.

64. Keilis-Borok, V.I., and A.A.Soloviev, Variations of trends of indicators describing complex systems: Change of scaling precursory to extreme events. Chaos, 2010, 20, 033104, doi:10.1063/1.3463438

65. Davis, C., V.Keilis-Borok, V.Kossobokov, and A.Soloviev, Advance prediction of the March 11, 2011 Great East Japan Earthquake: A missed opportunity for disaster preparedness. International Journal of Disaster Risk Reduction, 2012, 1: 17-32.

Books

V. I. Keilis-Borok and A. A. Soloviev (eds), Nonlinear Dynamics of the Lithosphere and Earthquake Prediction. Springer-Verlag, Berlin-Heidelberg, 2003, 337 p.

V.I.Keilis-Borok. 1960. Interferential Surface Waves. Ac. Sci. USSR. Moscow. 194 p. (in Russian)

ACKNOWLEDGEMENTS

I wish to thank all the contributors to this book, as well as all those people who were close to V. Keilis-Borok and whose friendship, collaborations, and other interactions left traces in his life. I am aware that he had connections with far more people than would be possible to even mention in this book. I am also aware that despite the many contacts with his friends and colleagues that I had over the years and established after his passing, I know only a fraction of those who knew him, and those who considered him a friend. Even if their names do not appear on the pages of this book, the spirit of these friendships is there and will continue to live on. I hope everyone who reads this book feels it the way I do.

My special thanks go to the International Center for Theoretical Physics, Trieste, Italy, whose generous contribution enabled the publication of this book.

Anna Kashina